BASEBALL'S GOLDEN AGE

THE PHOTOGRAPHS OF CHARLES M. CONLON

BASEBALL'S GOLDEN AGE

THE PHOTOGRAPHS OF CHARLES M. CONLON

By Neal McCabe and Constance McCabe

Harry N. Abrams, Inc., Publishers

Hi Mom

I ain't a bad looking guy in the White Sox uniform Al.
I will have my picture taken and send you boys some.

Jack Keefe
from Ring Lardner's *You Know Me Al*

Editor: Sharon AvRutick
Designer: Carol Robson

Library of Congress Cataloging-in-Publication Data

Conlon, Charles Martin.
    Baseball's golden age: the photographs of Charles M. Conlon/by
Constance McCabe and Neal McCabe.
        p.   cm.
        ISBN 0-8109-3130-3
        1. Baseball—History—Pictorial works.   2. Baseball—United
States—History—Pictorial works.   I. McCabe, Constance.   II. McCabe, Neal.
III. Title.
        GV862.5.C66   1993
        796.357'0973—dc20
                                                                93-187
                                                                CIP

In association with *The Sporting News* and with the cooperation of
Major League Baseball Properties, Inc.

Photographs copyright © 1993 The Sporting News Publishing
Co., St. Louis, MO, and are used with permission of THE
SPORTING NEWS.

Text copyright © 1993 Constance McCabe and Neal McCabe

Printed and bound in Japan

The photographs reproduced in this book were printed by Constance
McCabe from the original negatives at Photo Preservation Services,
Inc., Alexandria, Virginia

Page 2:

Cleveland Naps vs.
New York Highlanders
Hilltop Park, New York City
May 18, 1912

New York base runner Bert Daniels
has just been thrown out at the plate
by Cleveland center fielder Shoeless
Joe Jackson. Catcher Ted Easterly
applies the tag as umpire Billy Evans
makes the call. Cleveland third baseman Ivy Olson looks on.

Charles M. Conlon: "From his van-
tage point twenty feet from the plate,
with slide drawn and accurate focus,
the photographer watched. About a
dozen feet from the goal the runner
dropped for his slide, and almost at the
same instant, as he slid forward, the
spikes on his shoes glistening in the
bright sun, the ball reached the catcher.
One quick sweep of the arm, and the
runner was touched. Through the
cloud of dust that arose as the runner's
feet tore up the earth, the umpire
looked and waved his decision. It was a
lightning play and so close that no mor-
tal man could say definitely or decisive-
ly which had reached the plate first, the
runner or the ball. The umpire called
the man out, as he saw the play, and
instantly there was an uproar."

Preface

During a transcontinental telephone conversation in the fall of 1990, my sister casually mentioned that her photographic preservation firm was working on a new project: "It's a collection of old baseball photographs owned by *The Sporting News*. We're duplicating 8000 original negatives, mainly glass plates, all taken by a man named Conlon." "Never heard of him," I replied. "His photographs are extraordinary," she persisted, "and you would recognize a lot of them. This collection is like a time machine: He photographed the same people year after year for decades, and as I print these negatives in the darkroom, the players seem to age before my eyes." She explained that it was impossible to send the photos to me because they were owned by *The Sporting News*, but that it would be worth my while to pay her a special visit, just to get a look at the Conlon Collection. This suggestion struck me as absurd: "I've seen lots of old baseball pictures," I reasoned. And that, I thought, was that.

Over the next few months, however, my sister brought up the subject again and again, ignoring my apathy and obtuseness. I was somewhat intrigued by her uncharacteristic enthusiasm for old baseball pictures, but I was certain that her claims were wildly exaggerated. At the end of the year, when I finally arrived in Washington, D.C., for the holidays, she insisted that I look at the photographs. I was not prepared for what I saw: Here were some of the same famous images I had seen in books since my childhood, as well as beautiful photographs entirely new to me. My sister read the look of amazement on my face: "That's what I've been trying to tell you!" she said, with a mixture of amusement and exasperation.

I was puzzled, and more than a little embarrassed: Charles M. Conlon was obviously a great American photographer, and I had never heard of him. My sister had the catalogue for a 1984 Conlon exhibition at the National Portrait Gallery; the biographical information in the catalogue was sketchy, and the pictures were not nearly as interesting as the assortment my sister had just shown me. "Is there a book on this guy?" I asked. "No," she said, "but there ought to be."

In 1930, *New York Telegram* sportswriter Joe Williams was astonished to discover that an elderly proofreader at his newspaper was responsible for "the greatest action picture ever taken on a ball field." His charming and nostalgic interview with Charles M. Conlon was almost certainly the first of the photographer's life. In 1937, *The Sporting News* published a second interview with Conlon, in which several passages from the 1930 interview were repeated verbatim.

When we began work on this book, these two brief articles were the only primary sources of information on Conlon. It was possible to reconstruct his photographic career, given his prolific and well-documented output, but the details of his life seemed to be essentially irretrievable: Could it be, we wondered, that a few amusing anecdotes were all he left behind to illuminate his life's work? Then, after a long and seemingly pointless search, we serendipitously stumbled upon a forgotten article entitled "The Base Ball Photographer," written by Conlon in 1913 for *The Photographic Times*, a magazine devoted to amateur photography. Unfortunately, despite a promising title and some fine photographs, this rambling essay turned out to consist mainly of the same anecdotes he would still be recounting a quarter of a century later. Then it dawned on us: If Conlon had been in the habit of making artistic pronouncements, he would never have wasted his time hanging around ballparks. Conlon's life is implicit in his work, and, to paraphrase one of his contemporaries, photography was his passion, and the search for good shots of ball players, his obsession.

This book is not a reference work. It is not an illustrated history of baseball. It is a collection of Charles M. Conlon's best baseball photographs. This means, for example, that Silk O'Loughlin was certain to be featured in the book, even though a fairly important question remained to be answered—namely, who was Silk O'Loughlin? As it turned out, he was one of the most interesting characters in the history of baseball, an umpire who should be in the Hall of Fame, but, since historians have generally ignored him, it took long hours at the microfilm reader to find this out. Such searches were tedious, but rewarding: Filler material buried in an ancient issue of *The Sporting News* suddenly became strange and wonderful, simply because it provided evidence of the existence of Charles M. Conlon; a yellowed and crumbling newspaper clipping gave a new and unexpected meaning to a Conlon photograph.

Christy Mathewson never mentioned the photographer in *Pitching in a Pinch* (1912), the splendid book he wrote in collaboration with New York sportswriter John N. Wheeler, but he did vividly describe the personalities that his friend was photographing contemporaneously. The quotes and anecdotes in our book were gleaned largely from such contemporary accounts of Conlon's world, but we are also indebted to Fred Lieb, Harold Seymour, Lawrence Ritter, Donald Honig, Robert W. Creamer, Charles C. Alexander, Eugene C. Murdock, Bill James, and Marc Okkonen, the writers whose standard works we have repeatedly consulted in order to better understand that long-lost place and time.

Acknowledgments

The authors wish to thank a number of friends and colleagues for their support, trust, encouragement, and advice.

Without the dedication and scholarship of Steve Gietschier, Director of Historical Records of *The Sporting News* and custodian of the Conlon Collection, this book could never have been written. His superbly detailed catalogue of Conlon's negatives gave order to a daunting, sprawling collection. His generosity was simply overwhelming: He allowed us unlimited access to the archives of *The Sporting News*. We have attempted to produce a book worthy of his faith in us.

Many highly skilled professionals helped in the preparation of the photographs and text: Mary Lynn Ritzenthaler introduced us to Mr. Gietschier; Karen Garlick was particularly supportive, and we have benefited from her literary and computer expertise; and Sarah Wagner worked on the conservation treatment of an original photographic plate and spent considerable time preparing the prints for reproduction. Others who gave their time and exceptional talents in preparation of the prints include: Nancy Reinhold, Judy Walsh, Steve Puglia, Barbara Lemmen, Vicki Toye, and Pamela Kirschner. Thanks also to Jan Clubb, David Leaf, Terry Wallis, Tom and Carol McCarthy, Tom Keith, Nina Masonson, Shelley Fletcher, Nina Graybill, and Bill Topaz for their professional and personal support during the book's production.

Stephen Small, Director of Photo Preservation Services, Inc., deserves our special thanks. He was always there as a photographic troubleshooter, as a provider of technical information and expertise, and as a friend and supporter. For all his help, we are truly indebted.

Several people provided invaluable assistance in tracking down the elusive Charles M. Conlon: Patricia Kelly, photo collection manager of the National Baseball Library, Cooperstown, New York; Michael Salmon and the library staff of the Amateur Athletic Foundation, Los Angeles, California; Neil Victor and Debra Powell of Sportsbooks, West Hollywood, California; Ralph L. Horton of the Horton Publishing Company, St. Louis, Missouri; and Richard Kraus of the Los Angeles Public Library.

Charles M. Conlon was entirely dependent on the people who consented to pose for him, and we would especially like to thank those ball players and their families who graciously responded to our inquiries about the photographer: Ethan Allen, Dick Bartell, Boze Berger, Stanley and Vicki Bordagaray, Lou Boudreau, Mace Brown, Dolph Camilli, Harry Craft, Frank Crosetti, Tony Cuccinello, Dom DiMaggio, Bobby Doerr, Bob Feller, Rick Ferrell, Gail Ferry, Mrs. Hal Finney, Charlie Gehringer, Mel Harder, Buddy Hassett, Alex Kampouris, Mark Koenig, Max Lanier, Mary Lavagetto, Al Lopez, Pinky May, Johnny Mize, Hugh Mulcahy, Hal Newhouser, Bill Nicholson, Claude Passeau, Billy Rogell, Hal Schumacher, Birdie Tebbetts, Cecil Travis, and Bill Werber.

Our special gratitude goes to Frances Smythe of the National Gallery of Art for taking the time to review our book proposal. She encouraged Paul Gottlieb to look at it, and he, in turn, made the publication of this book possible. It has been a pleasure to work with our editor, Sharon AvRutick, and our book designer, Carol Robson, both of whom have been infinitely patient with a pair of rookie authors.

"The Base Ball Photographer"

The game which seems to breathe the restless spirit of American life, that calls for quick action and quicker thinking, that seems characteristic of a great nation itself, is baseball.

CHARLES M. CONLON

1913

When the World Series ended, he folded up his camera and waited for Opening Day. He had photographed everyone at the ballpark: players, managers, coaches, umpires, owners, visiting celebrities, wives, and children. Scores of fragile glass negatives, all meticulously identified in his neat hand, had been printed by the photographer in his home darkroom in preparation for their publication in the *Spalding Base Ball Guide*, the "Official Chronicle of America's National Game." In the winter, the editors combined his photographs in montages of ball players batting and throwing, leaping and catching. Row upon row of celebrated faces grinned and glared. On every page, two inconspicuous words appeared: "CONLON PHOTOS." When the spring came, he was back at the ballpark, ready to begin again.

He was not a professional photographer. He was not even a sports photographer. Yet Charles Martin Conlon was the greatest baseball photographer who ever lived, a newspaper proofreader who documented the golden age of baseball in his spare time. Today, his thousands of photographs form the basis of the unmatched collections of *The Sporting News* and the Baseball Hall of Fame. His images have become American icons, but their creator has vanished with barely a trace, his life's work submerged in the vast, anonymous pictorial heritage of baseball.

He was born in Albany, New York, in November 1868, at the same time that players were being recruited in Cincinnati, Ohio, for the first all-professional baseball team, the Red Stockings. During his childhood, there was a short-lived National League franchise in nearby Troy, New York, but the sport played no part in the young Conlon's life: "Baseball interested me," he recalled, "but it did not bother me to the extent that I would take a day off to see a game. You see, it was Albany. Perhaps if it had been New York, or some other city in the National League, it would have been different. I went into the printing business."

Conlon was employed by a local newspaper, the *Troy Press*, in the 1890s, but at the turn of the century he headed for the big city, where he found work at the *New York Evening Telegram*. The editor of the *Telegram*'s sports page was John B. Foster, who also served as the assistant editor of the annual *Spalding Base Ball Guide*. The *Spalding Guide* and its junior counterpart, the *Reach Guide*, were basically promotional tools for their respective sporting-goods companies, but they were indispensable to any true fan. These pocket-size baseball compendiums contained the most up-to-date rules of the game, complete statistics and detailed summaries of the previous season, schedules for the upcoming season, essays, editorials, and hundreds of photographs. Since 1881, the *Spalding Guide* had been edited by the venerable Henry Chadwick, a baseball authority who had seen his first game in 1856 while working as the cricket reporter for the *The New York Times*. His dedication to baseball during the next five decades had helped make the sport America's national pastime, but by 1904, the "Father of Base Ball" was seventy-nine years old, and he was grooming John B. Foster to take his place as editor of the *Guide*. "I came to know Foster very well," said Conlon. "He came to know about my hobby—taking pictures. He said to me one day, 'Charley, they need pictures of ball players for the *Guide*, and there is no reason why you can't take pictures of the players, as well as landscapes. It will be a good pickup for you, and it will be something for a day off.'"

In the spring of 1904, the thirty-five-year-old hobbyist brought his camera to the Polo Grounds, the ballpark of the New York Giants. This was not as ordinary an event as it seems to us today, when spectators take their cameras to baseball stadiums every day, when every team holds an annual promotional event called Camera Day, which allows fans to take close-up pictures of their favorite players on the field. Before the turn of the century, few photographers were interested in dragging their heavy camera equipment to anything as insignificant as a baseball game. Furthermore, their thick glass negatives were incapable of capturing the speed and excitement of the sport. The photographic record of that time consequently consists almost entirely of ball

Marge and Charles Conlon, c. 1909

Charles M. Conlon, 1935

"Of course I remember Charles Conlon," says Ethan Allen, a major-league outfielder and frequent Conlon subject. "The only problem I have is seeing his picture without a camera in his hands."

players in lifeless poses: young men in uniform with hair neatly combed and arms folded sitting together in frozen tableaux. There were primitive attempts to simulate the excitement of the game. One player would stand against a cheap studio backdrop, holding his hands together beneath a ball suspended on a wire; another would lie down on the floor with arms outstretched, pretending to slide. Charles M. Conlon saw other possibilities.

He had the field to himself. He stopped the star pitcher of the Giants outside the ballpark and persuaded him to pose. He assembled the Giants for a casual team portrait while laughing fans looked on. He took his camera out on the diamond to capture the players at their positions, and the players apparently enjoyed it as much as he did. He approached visiting players after the game and they, too, posed for the amateur photographer. He then paid a visit to the upstart New York Highlanders at their new American League ballpark.

Conlon's first baseball photographs were simple snapshots, often poorly framed and out of focus, in which a player's eyes were usually lost in the shadow cast by the bill of his cap. In some pictures, even the player's cap was barely visible against the sky, and the darkroom novice "improved" such photographs by crudely scratching the contours of the cap directly into the negative. (Fortunately, only a few of these early negatives were mutilated by the photographer; see page 180 for his least disastrous attempt at retouching.) Despite Conlon's shaky, nearly nonexistent technique, his first efforts were impressive. Today they seem almost miraculous: Ball players from another era are standing in the sunshine of the twentieth century. Some of these men are plainly amused by the photographer's attentions, and some are posing grudgingly, but in all of these portraits we can glimpse an evanescent moment in history, the dawning of baseball's golden age.

By the summer of 1904, Conlon's first uncredited photographs were appearing occasionally in the *New York Telegram*. His uncredited team photo of the Giants was printed in *The Sporting News* that fall. His portrait of pitcher Christy Mathewson was published in the 1905 *Spalding Guide* the next spring, but it was severely cropped, buried amid a sea of stilted studio poses, and, worse yet, credited to another photographer. Over the next few years, while talented photographers such as Francis P. Burke, Paul Thompson, W. M. Van der Weyde, and Louis Van Oeyen were beginning to produce their own remarkable player portraits, Conlon's pictures continued to appear haphazardly and anonymously.

In April 1908, however, the "Father of Base Ball" breathed his last, and John B. Foster succeeded him as editor of the *Spalding Guide*.

Foster's industrious protégé was the primary beneficiary of this change. By 1909, Conlon's credited photographs were dominating the *Spalding Base Ball Guide*; by 1911, they filled the *Reach Base Ball Guide*. For the next thirty years, he would be the principal photographer for both publications.

Photography was changing rapidly in the first decade of the twentieth century. It was now easier for a photographer to stop motion with the faster glass plates becoming available, and Conlon soon became fascinated with the possibilities of action photography. Around 1906, he began to take his camera onto the field during games: "The favorite position was about fifteen or twenty feet back of first or third," he recalled in 1913, "though occasionally the photographer would be seen hovering around home plate when the conditions of the game pointed to a possible play there. Through familiarity with the game he could usually tell where a slide was likely to occur."

There was a complicating factor: "The camera man was in constant danger from hard-hit drives. Camera in hand, he was not always in position to move rapidly, and the rifle-shot speed with which the ball frequently was driven toward him gave little opportunity to get out of range. Aside from countless narrow escapes, I was seriously injured twice. On one occasion, less than half an hour after I had assisted in caring for a brother photographer who was hit in the head by a batted ball, a vicious drive down the first base line caught me just above the ankle, and I was unable to walk for a couple of weeks." In 1937, Conlon revealed the culprit's identity: "Years ago, while I was off first, John Titus of the Phillies cut one down my way and struck me in the right ankle. It still hurts."

There were other risks in this war zone: "Larry Doyle was the biggest problem. The second baseman of the Giants had a habit of throwing his bat. It endangered players and picture men. [Giant manager John] McGraw saw me get a close shave one day from a Doyle bat, and ordered Larry to tie the stick to his wrist with a thong."

Besides being hazardous to a photographer's health, the action photo was the controversial forerunner of today's instant replay: "One day the Giants were playing the Cubs," Conlon recalled. "Oh, those were the games, and that was the *rivalry!* The Giants lost on a decision at the plate. The umpire called the man out, and I thought he was safe. I snapped the play. McGraw came out raving and called the umpire plenty. Tom Lynch, president of the National League, suspended Mac for three days and fined him. We reproduced the picture in the *Telegram* and it showed that the player had been safe by a stride. The umpire had his attention directed toward it in no kind or courteous manner the following day. The howl went up plenty. Lynch was in a very tough spot, but he settled the whole thing with an order barring cameramen from the field."

This 1910 ruling was immediately protested by *The Sporting News*: "Base ball photos, hot off the griddle, illustrating plays you have seen yourself, or which you revile yourself for missing, are becoming one of the most valuable and remunerative methods of keeping alive the interest in the real fans, and arousing a spirit of restless inquisitiveness among the backsliders which nothing but a fresh peep at a hot series on the home grounds will satisfy. At from twenty-five to seventy-five cents per peep to the financial improvement of the club, this free and unsolicited advertising is not to be despised. Professional base ball is not a necessity, it is an amusement enterprise essentially, based on sporting principles. Public—and newspaper—support and interest are absolutely necessary to the preservation of the enterprise. Whereof is the foolishness of T. Lynch? The action photo in base ball has come to stay, and will be long in the land after T. Lynch has been gathered to his fathers."

When he wasn't fending off vicious line drives or irate umpires, the exacting Conlon was waiting for just the right photograph. Even in the late innings of this action-packed ballgame, he had still not achieved a satisfactory shot: "One afternoon at the Polo Grounds, inning after inning passed, but without a picture. It was 10–2, in favor of the Giants. In the seventh inning, I was standing off third, and McGraw smiled, 'Charley, no picture today, what?' I complained bitterly and said I'd have to go back to the office without even a single shot to show for a whole day's work. 'I'll give you a picture,' he said. 'Be ready.' [Giant shortstop Al] Bridwell doubled to start the Giant half. Remember, it was 10–2. McGraw suddenly gave Brid the steal sign. Down came the shortstop, after a preliminary look of inquiry and amazement. He was nipped, and the picture was a corker. 'It was the best slide you ever made in your life—for the picture man,' McGraw grinned. Brid understood. The baseball writers discussed the play at some length in their stories and wondered if Brid had gone down on his own, and whether he or McGraw had had a brainstorm. What the writers did not know was the plight of the cameraman—me—without a picture. Managers have been swell to me, but John McGraw was in a class by himself."

Although Conlon took hundreds of action photos, only a handful of these negatives survive. One of them is his 1909 photograph of a sliding Ty Cobb (page 26): "It was not printed the next day," recalled Conlon in 1937. "It did not appear until the *Spalding Guide* came out the following spring." In fact, this astounding photograph was not published in the *Spalding Guide* until the spring of 1912, two and a half years after it was taken. When it finally did appear—misdated in the *Guide*—it was immediately recognized as something out of the ordinary: "A number of scenes of plays taken during the progress of the past season are given," said the reviewer for *Sporting Life*, "one of Ty Cobb making one of his characteristic slides being especially noteworthy as a remarkable example of snapshot photography." A black blob purporting to be a baseball was later added to the picture, and this egregious disfigurement of Conlon's most famous photograph has since been reproduced thousands of times. Fortunately, the negative was left untouched: The entire original image is offered here for the first time.

Action photography was the most exciting part of Conlon's work, but the pictures he took before the game constitute his true legacy, a profusion of breathtaking images as remarkable for their beauty as for the very fact that they exist at all. In his exquisite player portraits, his distinctive batting practice photos, and his innumerable photographs of players throwing a baseball and swinging a bat, Conlon systematically documented a strange and elegant world that was disappearing even as he took each picture, a world we can see today only because the photographer was awake to the dreams that surrounded him. Conlon had no artistic pretensions—he would remain a full-time proofreader at the *Telegram*—yet he steadily amassed a staggering body of work, at once delicate and powerful, by simply honoring John B. Foster's original request: "Charley, they need pictures of ball players for the *Guide*."

Pregame photography was not nearly as dangerous as taking action photos during a game, but Conlon was still dodging foul balls and errant throws as he wandered through the relaxed anarchy of batting and fielding practice. While ball players jogged, stretched, chatted, and scanned the stands for pretty faces, he carried his large Graflex camera, along with his cumbersome supply of glass negatives. (From 1904 until 1915, Conlon used a 5×7-inch format, and from 1916 until 1934 he used a 4×5-inch format. In the last years of his career, he was able to dispense with glass negatives, switching to 4×5-inch sheet film.) Burying his head in the hood of his camera, the part-time photographer worked quickly, and in a matter of minutes he could take a year's worth of photos of an entire team: As one player after another poses for the camera, we can often see the same fan, or fans, shifting in the grandstand. Conlon further expedited his work in 1913, when he settled on the background that became a constant element in his portraits for the next thirty years, the dugout roof. Haste is evident in many of his photographs: Conlon never fully mastered the mysteries of focus, and he often guessed at exposure times because of the tricky and undependable natural light at the ballpark. But at his best, Conlon created photographs of such perfection that it is difficult to believe that they were taken under such unlikely conditions.

By 1920, Charles M. Conlon had become, de facto, the official photographer of baseball. He was the staff photographer for *Baseball Magazine*. He had his own logo in the *Spalding* and *Reach Base Ball Guides*. His pictures were sold on baseball cards and posters, they advertised soda pop and shotguns, they appeared in the *New York Telegram* and *The Sporting News*, and they illustrated baseball manuals and textbooks. When the autobiography of his old friend John McGraw was published in 1923, it naturally featured Conlon photographs. And whenever the Yankees or Giants won the pennant in the 1920s and '30s, virtually an annual event in those years, Conlon provided the player portraits for the World Series souvenir programs.

Strangely, even as his photographs inundated the baseball world, his name rarely appeared with his work in print. His pictures had long been accumulating in the files of photo agencies such as Underwood and Underwood, where individual photographers inevitably remained nameless, and, except for the *Guides*, where his artless logo evolved by the late thirties into a twisted Deco grotesque, the photographer was at the mercy of layout artists who rarely chose to acknowledge his contributions. The posters sold by *Baseball Magazine* bore his name, but his pictures were seldom credited in the *New York Telegram* or *The Sporting News*, and they were never credited in the World Series programs, on baseball cards, or in advertisements. Conlon seems to have been indifferent to his relative obscurity, perhaps because he knew that in the world of journalism it had long been self-evident that a baseball photo was a Conlon photo.

It is interesting to note that Conlon, who had unlimited access to every sporting event in New York, never chose to document any sport but baseball. He did take a few snapshots at the 1922 Davis Cup tennis tournament, but these perfunctory photographs pale even in comparison to the pictures he took of his birds, Tottie and Monkey, and his cats, Buddy and Kiddo. He seems never to have been an avid sports fan, yet he was drawn to the world of baseball: From his first day at the ballpark, Conlon felt at home, and his best portraits of ball players are as warm and intimate, as direct and revealing, as a man's pictures of his family and friends. Conlon looked back on his decades of baseball photography with satisfaction and gratitude: "No man ever did a bigger favor than John B. Foster did for me that morning in 1904. It wasn't the money—that's negligible. But the fun I have had, the days in the open, the associations, the confidences I have enjoyed—well, you can't buy those things."

By 1938, Conlon was sixty-nine years old, and he finally began to slow down. He made fewer trips from his home in Englewood, New Jersey, to the ballparks across the Hudson River. He no longer took every player's portrait, and in 1939, he actually shared photo credits in the *Guides* for the first time in decades. By this time, hundreds of energetic young baseball photographers were crowding the old man out of *Baseball Magazine* and *The Sporting News*. In 1940, the *Reach Guide* merged with the *Spalding Guide*, and after John B. Foster's death in 1941, the *Guide* ceased publication entirely. In 1942, by now retired from his newspaper job and deprived of the main outlets for his work, the seventy-three-year-old photographer nevertheless took his camera out to the ballpark for a few last pictures.

His valedictory photographs were taken at the end of the golden age of baseball: Ball players were now leaving to fight in World War II, and the sport would enter the modern era upon their return. Conlon would never photograph Jackie Robinson, just as he had never photographed Satchel Paige, Josh Gibson, Cool Papa Bell, or any of the other Negro League players denied a chance to play in the big leagues because of the institutionalized racism of baseball. Had the major leagues been integrated during his lifetime, Conlon would certainly have made portraits of black players, just as he photographed Native Americans Jim Thorpe and Chief Meyers, members of a minority magnanimously deemed "acceptable" by the bigoted club owners. Conlon's work was a product of his life and times, and the fact of this incalculable loss remains: There are no black faces in Conlon's baseball gallery.

When his wife, Marge, passed away, Conlon gave up photography and went back to Troy, New York, where he died in 1945 at the age of seventy-six. His original negatives had already been acquired by *The Sporting News*, but most of his original photographs remained in the files of his old newspaper, which had become the *New York World-Telegram* in 1931. When it ceased publication in 1967, Conlon's photographs were acquired by the Baseball Hall of Fame.

Many of Conlon's subjects are still alive and well, but few have any memories of him. Bill Werber, a major-league third baseman who Conlon photographed many times, explains: "I have no recollection of Charles Conlon. Lest you deem me to be on the stupid side, a word in defense of my position. These photographers were very zealous at their profession and several of them would be in and around the diamond areas of these parks every day. When asked to pose for a picture, we were happy to accommodate, but it was never necessary to ask: 'What is your name?' 'Whom are you taking pictures for?' Consequently, folks were taking pictures in Boston, Washington, and St. Louis, and I never bothered to ask for identity." First baseman Buddy Hassett points out another problem: "It's tough trying to remember fifty years ago."

Today, Conlon is remembered fondly, if a little vaguely, by the few ball players who can remember him at all. Hall of Fame catcher Al Lopez and Detroit Tiger shortstop Billy Rogell are among those who can recall Conlon, and they both use the same word to describe him: "gentleman." Perhaps this helps to explain the disparity between Conlon's monumental achievement and his posthumous anonymity. He blended into a crowd of cameramen, content to let his work speak for itself.

Conlon's name has never appeared in any history of American photography, and he is scarcely noted even in the vast literature of baseball, but it is difficult to overstate the significance of his work. His most famous photographs are, quite simply, the most famous baseball photographs ever taken. Turn over any historic photo in the files of the Baseball Hall of Fame, and, more likely than not, it will be stamped "Charles M. Conlon—*Evening Telegram*, New York." His photographs have appeared in hundreds of baseball books, including such classic works as *Eight Men Out* and *The Glory of Their Times*, but even the most ordinary Conlon photos are valuable documents, offering fascinating data on everything from uniforms, bats, and gloves to the advertisements on the outfield fence. In 1937, Conlon had some idea of his work's importance: "I could do quite a book around those hundreds of fine pictures I still possess, but," he wondered, "how many of the present generation would know anything about the men depicted? They tell me that there are players in the big leagues who don't know a thing about the heroes of the past." No effort was made to publish such a collection during Conlon's lifetime.

Among Conlon's historic photographs was the first picture of Giant catcher Roger Bresnahan wearing his new invention, shin guards: "When he put them on that day I thought he was joking," recalled Conlon. "He looked as if he were made up for a masquerade, and I remember that the fans jeered him. They waved handkerchiefs, whistled, and called him 'Percy.'" The photograph appeared the next year in the 1908 *Spalding Guide*, but the negative is nowhere to be found. Hundreds of other important negatives, such as the studies of Three-Finger Brown's pitching hand, Babe Ruth's rookie photo, and dozens of World Series action shots, are similarly missing. The photographer solved this mystery in 1937 with an explanation that will chill any fan's blood: "Some years ago, I found that my plates were running me out of the house, so I destroyed hundreds of them. Perhaps it was a mistake, but where would I have kept them? It is possible that had we had a Cooperstown museum at the time, they would have found a

haven there." In fact, the photographer destroyed thousands and thousands of negatives, apparently at random. Had it not been for the farsighted editors of *The Sporting News*, who were no doubt horrified by Conlon's tale, all of his negatives might have been lost.

The Conlon Collection of *The Sporting News* consists of the photographer's 8000 remaining original negatives. To be in the presence of these negatives is as close as we will come to experiencing the presence of Christy Mathewson, Wee Willie Keeler, or any of the other early ball players photographed by Conlon. There are motion pictures of some of these players, but they are fragmentary and fleeting: A jerky film clip of Christy Mathewson playing catch for the newsreel camera in 1906 has become ridiculous, while Conlon's 1904 negative of Mathewson will forever evoke the pitcher's hauteur and grace. It is remarkable that it is possible to hold in one's hand an object that is, in essence, a piece of the past, magically capturing the memory of an otherwise lost or forgotten moment: Cy Young warming up at Hilltop Park, Shoeless Joe Jackson throwing out a runner at the plate, Ginger Beaumont squinting in the sun.

No one considered Conlon's photographs works of art in his lifetime. Large and obtrusive identifying marks were routinely scribbled on his negatives, apparently by photo editors at the *Spalding Guide* and *Baseball Magazine*. His early 5×7-inch plates usually contained far more picture information than could be squeezed onto the already overcrowded pages of the *Spalding Guide*, and the prints the photographer made from these negatives were often heavily cropped. Today, these original prints are an invaluable resource, but many were retouched and irreparably damaged in newspaper offices decades ago, and most are now severely worn and creased. The Conlon photos we are used to seeing in books are poorly reproduced copies of these scratched and overused prints, and they look like they were taken sixty, seventy, or eighty years ago. The photographs reproduced in the present volume were all newly printed from the original negatives, and most of them look like they were taken one afternoon during a recent home stand.

Conlon deserves to be ranked with the acknowledged masters of twentieth-century documentary photography, Eugène Atget and Walker Evans. All of these men were intuitive, self-taught photographers who collected the world around them, who found unexpected beauty in ordinary places, and who then preserved that beauty in straight, unadorned images. Topsy Hartsel (page 192), his baseball bat poised on a distant coffee cup, is as stately, dignified—and absurd—as Atget's Parisian baker proudly holding an enormous loaf of bread. Conlon's portrait of Bill Dickey (page 193) is as stark and haunting as

Walker Evans' portrait of an Alabama sharecropper's wife. But while Evans was aware of Atget and learned from his work, Conlon was an American original, even closer to Atget in time, in spirit, and in practice. Like Atget, Conlon spent decades in a narrowly circumscribed environment, working outside the photographic establishment, oblivious to and unaffected by artistic trends. And, like Atget, he left us the definitive visual record of the place he loved.

The ballpark was Conlon's universe, an inexhaustible source of unforgettable images: a catcher's mangled hand, a madman kicking up his heels, an umpire lost in thought. He documented baseball obsessively at a time when critics of photography—had they known of his existence—would have questioned his sanity for taking thousands of photographs of so trivial and ephemeral a subject. In recent years, writers have wondered why serious photographers have never been attracted to baseball. After all, they point out, baseball has never had a photographer capable of capturing the magic of the game with an artist's eye. They need to be reminded that there was indeed such a photographer at the field of dreams. His name was Charles M. Conlon.

Christy Mathewson
1904 New York Giants

He was sometimes accused of arrogance and aloofness, yet here the greatest pitcher in baseball obligingly poses for an amateur photographer in the Polo Grounds carriage park (the turn-of-the-century equivalent of the parking lot). The white posts in the distance marked the end of the playing field and were used to rope off overflow crowds. The elevation behind the ballpark is Coogan's Bluff, where fans could go to view the game without a ticket.

This is the first baseball photograph Conlon ever took. It illustrated Mathewson's "body swing" (windup) in *How to Pitch* (1905), an instructional booklet for boys edited by Conlon's mentor, John B. Foster.

Jimmy Gralich Imitating Matty
c. 1913

Mathewson was the idol of every young baseball fan, in many ways the very first sports role model. Here Conlon's young nephew faithfully reproduces Matty's familiar windup. Conlon arranged a meeting between Jimmy and Matty at the Polo Grounds, where the awestruck boy was able to shake his hero's hand.

Billy Sullivan
1911 Chicago White Sox

On August 24, 1910, this man caught a
ball dropped by Ed Walsh from the
top of the Washington Monument—on
the twenty-fourth try. Here, wearing
his customary extra-heavy mitt, he re-
creates one of those twenty-three earlier attempts for Conlon.

Billy Sullivan was Ed Walsh's
catcher during the spitballer's greatest
years, and no less a critic than Cy
Young gave Sullivan the credit for
turning Walsh into a real pitcher. In
1909, dissatisfied with the cumbersome inflated chest protectors worn by
catchers at the turn of the century,
Billy designed and patented the Sullivan Body Protector, the flexible chest
protector that, with minor modifica-
tions, is still in use today.

Ed Walsh
c. 1913 Chicago White Sox

Walsh was one of the greatest pitchers of the dead-ball era, the man who once won forty games in a season and who still holds the major-league record for career earned run average. While he did not invent the spitball, Walsh was certainly its most brilliant exponent. Here he demonstrates his trademark grip for Conlon.

Despite Walsh's phenomenal success with the spitter, White Sox manager Fielder Jones recommended that the pitch be outlawed: "In my opinion, the spitball is doing a great injury to the game. In the first place, it is not natural. In the second place, it is not cleanly. Lots of people do not like to go out to the park and watch a pitcher slobbering all over the ball. Thirdly, the use of the spitball lengthens the games, as pitchers who depend upon the spitball consume so much time applying the moisture."

Big Ed offered this expert rebuttal: "You don't use a big gob of saliva. Most people have the impression that the ball is soggy when you throw the spitter. It isn't. Two wet fingers are all that is necessary to throw the spitter. You don't have to use your mouth to load it. Perspiration will serve the same purpose." Case closed.

Mike Donlin
1912 Pittsburgh Pirates

In 1906, *The Sporting News* condemned Mike Donlin as a "degenerate" whose "batting ability has kept him in a manly profession in spite of his record as a rowdy and a woman-beater." He had already served a prison term for his drunken assault on an actress in 1902 and was now charged with terrorizing passengers on a train, but Turkey Mike (nicknamed for his flamboyant strut) had also led the Giants to the 1905 world championship, and the New York fans loved Donlin as they would one day love Babe Ruth, forgiving him all his sins.

Mike married vaudeville actress Mabel Hite in 1906 and joined her on stage, becoming such a success that he retired from baseball in 1907, at the very peak of his brilliant playing career. He returned to the Giants in 1908 but left baseball for show business again in 1909 and 1910. The peripatetic Donlin became a Pirate in 1912, exclaiming: "Gee, but it's great to be with a real live team again!"

When his playing career ended, Mike became a movie actor: "I'm here to knock Hollywood right into the Pacific Ocean. Watch Mike Donlin burn up them films." But aside from a small role in his pal Buster Keaton's classic *The General* and a few lines of dialogue in Mae West's *She Done Him Wrong*, Donlin's film career consisted mainly of bit parts in B gangster movies with titles like *Born Reckless* and *Hot Curves*.

Garry Herrmann and Ban Johnson
Fenway Park, Boston, 1914

The all-powerful dictators of baseball survey their domain at the 1914 World Series. Johnson (right), the "Czar of Baseball," was the founder and president of the American League. Herrmann (left), his servile courtier and drinking buddy, was the owner of the Cincinnati Reds and chairman of the National Commission, the governing body of baseball until the Black Sox scandal put it out of business.

John McGraw
1912 New York Giants

In this study of the pensive Giant manager, Conlon may have taken the very first action shot of a player spitting in the dugout (extreme left).

Christy Mathewson: "Ball-players are very superstitious about the bats. Did you ever notice how the clubs are all laid out in a neat, even row before the bench and are scrupulously kept that way by the bat boy? If one of the sticks by any chance gets crossed, all the players will shout: 'Uncross the bats! Uncross the bats!'"

Honus Wagner
1912 Pittsburgh Pirates

Conlon took close-up shots of all the great players demonstrating their batting grips, but only Honus Wagner flexed his muscles for the camera. In 1912, Mike Donlin made this observation to a New York sportswriter: "Do you know why Hans Wagner is playing better ball than ever this year? The answer is easy. The big Dutchman's hands are growing bigger and his arms are getting longer all the time." Contemporaries always remarked on the size of Wagner's extremities, some even comparing him to a gorilla.

Wagner was the first batter ever to have his signature branded on a Louisville Slugger. In 1912, John McGraw told a Pittsburgh sportswriter: "You can have your Cobbs, your Lajoies, your Chases, your Bakers, and all the rest, but I'll take Wagner. He does *every-thing* better than the ordinary star can do any *one* thing. He is the most wonderful ball player who ever lived." Even the arrival of Babe Ruth a few years later could not change McGraw's appraisal of Wagner.

← Hack Wilson
1924 New York Giants

Wilson was never more than a part-time outfielder when he played for the Giants, and in 1925 he was demoted to their Toledo farm club. During this routine transaction the Giants' front office made the worst clerical error in the history of baseball: Wilson was left unprotected in the minor-league draft, and the Chicago Cubs were able to steal a future Hall of Famer. The blunder never ceased to plague John McGraw, especially when Hack led the Cubs to the 1929 National League pennant.

This startling photograph appeared on the cover of the 1928 edition of *Who's Who in Baseball.*

Dizzy Dean
1934 St. Louis Cardinals

In the midst of his greatest season, Dizzy has just thrown his blazing fastball for Conlon's benefit. He would go on to win thirty games and lead the Gas House Gang to victory in the World Series.

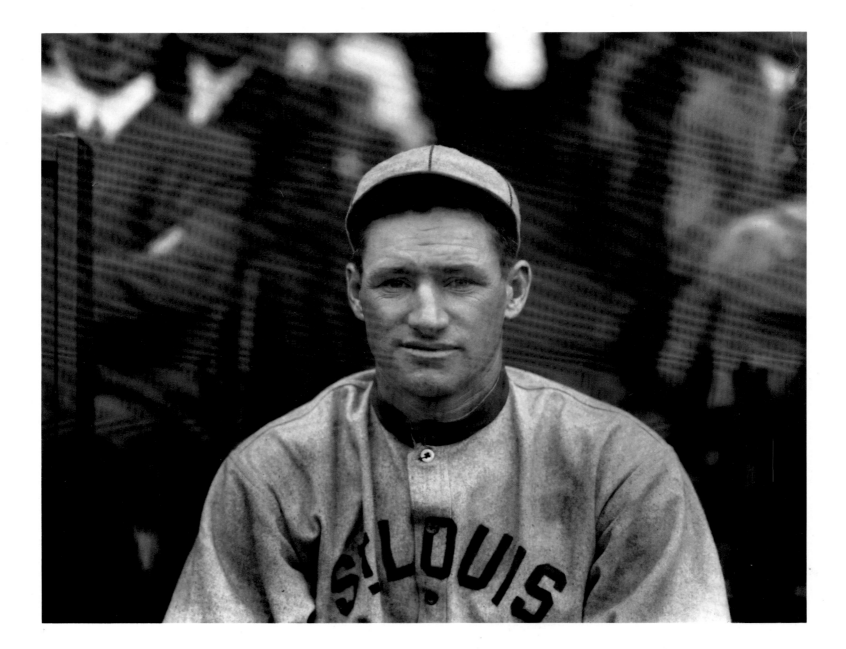

Jimmy Austin
1912 St. Louis Browns

The Original Pepper Kid earned his nickname because he never stopped hustling, in spite of his modest talents: "He may not hit and he may not field and he may not throw, but by jimminy he will liven 'em up," said Lee Fohl, one of Austin's managers with the Browns. When Branch Rickey was named manager of the Browns in 1913, a slight problem arose: "When I was a boy in college," explained Rickey, "I promised my mother that I would never play ball on Sunday, or go near a ballgame. I regard that promise as sacred and I intend to keep it as long as I live." His solution was to name Jimmy Austin as the team's Sunday manager. One major problem remained, however: The Browns were terrible regardless of who their manager was.

Frances Willard Chandler
and Frank Willard Chandler
Yankee Stadium, 1942

The 1938 meeting between Spud Chandler and his future bride might have been scripted in Hollywood: He was a sore-armed Yankee pitcher and she was a beautiful blonde with appendicitis. They met in the hospital and fell in love while recuperating from their respective operations. The stork brought the Chandlers a little Spud in the summer of '41.

Wee Willie Keeler
1909 New York Highlanders

"Keeler is as superstitious as a crap-shooter," reported *The Sporting News* in 1906. "He swears by the teeth of the mask-carved horse chestnut that he always carries with him as a talisman that he invariably dreams of it the night before when he is going to boot one—muff an easy fly ball, that is to say—in the meadow on the morrow. 'All of us fellows in the outworks have got just so many of them a season to drop and there's no use trying to buck against fate.' " Here, in one of Conlon's most famous photographs, Keeler poses solemnly in the meadow at Hilltop Park, his sad eyes gazing skyward with a look of foreboding and resignation.

In his prime, 5′4¹/₂″ Wee Willie was the most consistent hitter in baseball and his forty-four-game hitting streak is unsurpassed in the National League to this day. His batting philosophy was elegant in its simplicity: "I hit 'em where they ain't."

Joe Martina
1924 Washington Senators

Oyster Joe, a 349-game winner in the minor leagues, made it to the majors for one mediocre season and actually pitched a scoreless inning in the 1924 World Series. Conlon caught him in his one brief shining moment of big-league glory, but, alas, Martina's teammates are teasing him as he takes an unaccustomed bow in the spotlight.

Martina is named as "The Ugliest Player of the 1920s" in *The Bill James Historical Baseball Abstract* (1986), with this photograph offered as incontrovertible evidence.

Bob Rhoads
1909 Cleveland Naps

Over the objections of his Amish parents, sixteen-year-old Barton Emery Rhoads became a professional baseball pitcher in 1896. When he came up to the big leagues with the Chicago Cubs in 1902, he changed his name to Bob in order to spare his family further humiliation, but his punning teammates dubbed him Dusty. Rhoads was a flop with the Cubs but became a successful starter for Cleveland, winning twenty-two games in 1906 and pitching a no-hitter in 1908. Unfortunately, after a poor year in 1909, he was traded back to the Cubs, whereupon he fled to Canada rather than play for his old team again.

Conlon's beautiful photograph appeared in the *New York Evening Telegram* in 1909 and served as the basis for two classic baseball cards, but Rhoads's defection from baseball rendered publication of this photograph in the 1910 *Spalding Guide* pointless. The negative was then filed away and forgotten for more than eight decades.

Lou Gehrig
1930 New York Yankees

Conlon customarily photographed a batter at the end of his swing, but he preferred to pose Gehrig in his batting stance, the better to display Lou's massive leg muscles, the product of his favorite winter pastime, speed skating. 1930 was one of Gehrig's greatest years: 41 home runs, 174 runs batted in, and a career-high 379 batting average.

Rogers Hornsby
1925 St. Louis Cardinals

In 1925, Rogers Hornsby won his sixth straight National League batting title and his second Triple Crown. His batting average plummeted twenty-one points from the previous year—and he still hit .403. Hornsby is, without question, the best right-handed hitter in the history of baseball, a man who never watched a movie during the season lest he adversely affect his preternaturally acute batting eye.

Bill Bergen
1911 Brooklyn Superbas

This man is, without question, the worst hitter in the history of baseball. His lifetime batting average was a truly pathetic .170, yet he was a valuable player throughout his eleven-year major-league career because of his extraordinary skill as a catcher. In 1906, a Pittsburgh sportswriter hinted at the source of Bill's unsteady batting eye and his bleary expression in this photograph: "Bergen is a fine catcher, and would be finer still but for his desire to live well. Out this way we have rumors that now and then Bergen is late reporting for duty, all because he met some friends who will invite him to have a bite to eat, etc. Not caring about being churlish, he accepts, and will look on life as a round of pleasure. Time will come when the Brooklyn man will get down to solid base ball playing and forget good things in the pleasure line." But that time never came. In 1911, Bill batted an abysmal .132, unacceptable even by his undemanding standards, and his big-league round of pleasure was over.

Ted Williams
1939 Boston Red Sox

The Kid made his big-league debut at Yankee Stadium on Opening Day in 1939, and the inevitable Charles M. Conlon was there to greet him, camera in hand. Williams knocked in 145 runs in 1939, leading the major leagues and setting the all-time rookie RBI mark.

Joe DiMaggio
1937 New York Yankees

In 1937, his second season with the Yankees, DiMaggio played in his first All-Star Game. He also appeared in his first movie, *Manhattan Merry-Go-Round*, but wisely kept his day job. He was completely unaffected by the dreaded sophomore jinx in 1937, hitting forty-six home runs and knocking in 167 runs, the highest totals of his career. Joe had the audacity to hold out for a hefty pay raise after this marvelous season, and in 1938 he was rewarded with boos from the fans. It took his epochal fifty-six-game hitting streak in 1941 to finally win them back.

Cy Young
1910 Cleveland Naps

This is the most famous picture ever taken of the winningest pitcher in baseball history. Young was forced to retire in the spring of 1912 because of a problem already apparent in Conlon's photograph: "My arm is as good as the day I came into the majors, but I'm too portly to get about. The boys know this and bunt on me. When the third baseman has to start doing my work it's time for me to quit."

Bob Feller
1938 Cleveland Indians

In 1932, Bill Feller built a ballpark on his Iowa farm because he knew that they would come. And they did, but it cost them twenty-five cents apiece for the privilege of watching his thirteen-year-old son pitch. In 1938, this pitching prodigy was in his third year in the majors, leading the league in strikeouts. By 1940, he was the best pitcher in baseball.

Al Simmons
1924 Philadelphia Athletics

In 1921, nineteen-year-old Al Simmons took pen in hand: "Dear Mr. Mack," he wrote, "I am an amateur ball player in Milwaukee and have played for the Right Laundry, Juneau, Stevens Point, and Iola teams. I would like to have a try-out with the Philadelphia Athletics, because I have heard and read so much about them and you. If you take me down South with you, I am sure I can make good."

"Dear Mr. Simmons," replied manager Connie Mack, "I appreciate your interest in my team and me but it is impossible for me to give you a try-out this season. I receive about 1000 similar requests every year." Thus, one of the greatest players in baseball history offered his services to the A's free of charge—and received a perfunctory rebuff. In 1924, Mack finally did acquire Simmons, but this time it cost him $50,000 in cash and players.

Al Simmons
1939 Cincinnati Reds

At thirty-seven, every ball player has the face he deserves. It is the 1939 World Series, and Al Simmons is watching his baseball life slip away. Once an MVP, a batting champion, a World Series hero, a superstar, he is now an ancient and embittered castoff playing for his fifth team in five years. Al's obsessive quest for his 3000th career hit proved futile—too many late nights took their toll.

Charlie Gehringer
1925 Detroit Tigers

When this kid from Fowlerville, Michigan, tried out for the Tigers in 1923, Ty Cobb was so impressed that he signed him up on the spot. Gehringer had just arrived in the majors to stay when Conlon took his photograph at the end of the 1925 season; the rookie's pained and wary expression would remain fixed throughout his brilliant career.

The folks from Fowlerville honored their self-effacing hometown hero with a Charlie Gehringer Day, during which he graciously accepted their gift of a beautiful set of right-handed golf clubs. Rather than embarrass his friends by pointing out that he was a lefty, Charlie quietly became an excellent right-handed golfer.

Charlie Gehringer
1934 Detroit Tigers

Nine years have passed, and the Mechanical Man is now the best second baseman in the major leagues, leading the Tigers to their first World Series appearance in twenty-five years. "He is a manager's dream," said Detroit manager Mickey Cochrane. "Gehringer arrives at the first of the season and says, 'Hello.' He goes along and hits something like .350, and at the end of the season, he says, 'Goodbye, see you next season.' "

Gehringer chose to remain a bachelor during his playing career so that he could care for his ailing mother. When he was elected to the Hall of Fame a few years after his mother's death, he strangely failed to attend his own induction ceremony. The mystery was solved with the announcement that Charlie had just eloped with his sweetheart.

Tim "Big City" Jordan
1910 Brooklyn Superbas

One winter day in 1908, Big City surveyed the Brooklyn ballpark, its frozen playing field converted into an enormous ice-skating rink, and mused: "Say, if I hit a home run now, wouldn't it travel?"

This slugging New York City native was enormously popular with the hometown fans and twice led the major leagues in home runs, yet he is forgotten today except for this famous Conlon image, one of the most graceful batting photographs ever taken. It is April 1910 at the Polo Grounds, the time and place of Jordan's one and only hit of the season, the last of his big-league career: a pinch-hit home run. The next month he would be exiled to the minors forever, the victim of a knee injury. Big City's replacement at first base was Jake Daubert, a rookie who made the Brooklyn fans forget about Jordan in a hurry.

Tim eventually found employment as a house detective at the Hotel Astor.

Jim Bottomley
1929 St. Louis Cardinals

Here is a pitcher's nightmare and a photographer's dream. Bottomley was the National League MVP in 1928, when he led the league in homers, triples, and RBIs. In 1924, he knocked in twelve runs in a single game, setting a major-league record that still stands today. Sunny Jim is immortalized in this classic Conlon portrait of a kindly man beaming under a crooked cap.

Jack Dunn
1904 New York Giants

This man discovered George Herman Ruth and signed him to his first professional contract on Valentine's Day, 1914. When the nineteen-year-old Ruth showed up for spring training, the other players began calling the childlike pitcher Dunnie's Babe, and the nickname stuck. Conlon snapped this picture when Dunn was a utility man playing out his career for his former Baltimore Oriole teammate John McGraw. When Dunn sold Ruth to the Red Sox in 1914, without offering him to the Giants, McGraw was so hurt by his old friend's betrayal that he never forgave him.

Joseph Lannin
Boston Red Sox Owner, c. 1914

On July 18, 1914, this man bought Babe Ruth for the grand total of $2900. The Canadian-born Lannin began his life in America at fifteen as a Boston bellhop, but by the time he bought the Red Sox in 1913 he owned hotels, apartments, and golf courses up and down the East Coast. The Red Sox won the World Series in both 1915 and 1916, but Lannin grew so weary of the business of baseball that he decided to quit while he was ahead, selling the team to theatrical producer Harry Frazee in December 1916. When Lannin threatened to foreclose on Fenway Park because of money still owed him in 1919, the irresponsible Frazee made the most momentous and short-sighted transaction in the history of baseball: He sold Babe Ruth to the New York Yankees, and "The Curse of the Bambino" was born. Since 1918 the Red Sox have never won a World Series, and Boston fans swear that the Babe is still having his revenge.

← Bill Carrigan
1915 Boston Red Sox

Nicknamed Rough as a young catcher, Carrigan was Babe Ruth's first and favorite major-league manager. He led the Red Sox to world championships in 1915 and 1916, before abruptly retiring to a banking career in Lewiston, Maine.

Carrigan occasionally played first base, and even then he wore his catcher's mitt.

Lefty Gomez →
1937 New York Yankees

This man coined the expression "gopher ball" and provided its etymology: "This is a very special delivery of mine. I throw the ball, and then the batter swings—and then it will go for three or four bases." Gomez is remembered today mainly for his self-deprecating wit, but he was the Yankees' pitching ace throughout the 1930s, with a 6–0 lifetime World Series record to prove it. This is an unusual photograph for Conlon in that he rarely photographed a pitcher in mid-windup and even more rarely tilted his camera for artistic effect.

Babe Ruth
1918 Boston Red Sox

In 1917, Babe Ruth won twenty-four games as a pitcher, but he was such a great hitter that the Red Sox decided to convert him into an outfielder. In 1918, he still pitched in twenty games, compiling a 13-7 record. Thus, when Ruth led the league in homers this year, he became the first and only pitcher to do so. Conlon was there to document the beginning of the Babe's batting ascendancy.

Babe Ruth
1922 New York Yankees

Ruth had two of his greatest seasons in 1920 and 1921, but 1922 was a catastrophe. He was suspended five times before the season ended, and batted an execrable .118 in the 1922 World Series. *The Sporting News* dubbed Ruth the "Exploded Phenomenon" and declared: "The baseball public is onto his real worth as a batsman and in future, let us hope, he will attract just ordinary attention."

Babe Ruth
1924 New York Yankees

Ruth bounced back in 1923 with a career-high batting average of .393. In 1924, he led the league in batting average and home runs, finishing second in RBIs. This was the closest Babe Ruth ever came to winning the Triple Crown.

Babe Ruth
1926 New York Yankees

In 1925, Babe Ruth had a miserable year, enduring "the bellyache heard round the world." Skeptics wondered if the thirty-one-year-old slugger was starting to slip. In 1926, however, he tore up the league, leading the Yankees to their first pennant since 1923. Here Conlon captures the Babe near the very peak of his career.

Babe Ruth
1934 New York Yankees

Ruth in his last and worst year with the Yankees. His skills had severely eroded, as Conlon's photograph makes disturbingly clear.

Helen Ruth with Daughter Dorothy Ruth and Nick Altrock
1925 Washington Senators

Helen Woodford was a sixteen-year-old waitress when she married a rookie pitcher named Babe Ruth. Little did she know that her husband would eventually become the nation's most notorious carouser and womanizer. By the time Conlon took this photograph, the Ruths' marriage was in ruins, although it would not end legally until Helen's death in a fire in 1929. Dorothy had been adopted by the couple in 1922.

Nick Altrock was a pitching star for the Chicago White Sox in the 1906 World Series. In later years, wearing his trademark crooked cap, Altrock performed a popular slapstick routine in ballparks throughout the country with Al Schacht, the Clown Prince of Baseball.

Jim Thorpe
1917 Cincinnati Reds

He was the greatest athlete of the
first half of the twentieth century,
but Jim Thorpe could not hit a
curveball. He was a sensational
college football player and the
winner of the pentathlon and
decathlon at the 1912 Olympics,
but he was stripped of his gold
medals when it was discovered
that he had played two summers
of professional baseball. Because
the National Football League did
not yet exist, Thorpe was forced
to put his athletic skills to work as
a baseball player. His major-league
career was little more than a pub-
licity stunt, except for one game in
1917: He knocked in the winning
run in the tenth inning of a classic
pitching duel in which the Reds'
Fred Toney and the Cubs' Hippo
Vaughn both pitched no-hitters
for the first nine innings.

Zeke Bonura
1939 New York Giants

Bonura was a gifted amateur athlete who won the javelin throw at the National AAU Track and Field Championships in 1925. "One day I was suiting up for a football game. I was a newcomer, so naturally the other fellows looked me over. One exclaimed, 'Look at that huge physique,' and ever since then I have been known as Zeke." He was also known as Bananas (because his father was a wealthy fruit wholesaler) and Banana Nose (see photo).

Zeke was oddly superstitious about his bats. They were always red on one side and white on the other because he insisted that they be cut from the center, or heart, of the tree. Conlon caught him as he performed a delicate procedure recommended by the makers of the Louisville Slugger: "Honing, preferably with a dry meat bone, closes the pores of the wood, hardens the bat's surface, prevents slivering and adds punch to hits." This well-groomed, albeit peculiar, bat helped Bonura to a lifetime batting average of .307.

Dazzy Vance
1933 St. Louis Cardinals

"Where did I get the nickname Dazzy? Well it has nothing to do with 'dazzling speed' as most fans believe. Back in Nebraska I knew a cowboy who, when he saw a horse, a gun or a dog that he liked would say, 'Ain't that a daisy,' only he would pronounce 'daisy' as 'dazzy.' I got to saying, 'Ain't that a dazzy,' and before I was eleven years old the nickname had been tacked on me."

Pitching for the Brooklyn Dodgers in the 1920s, Vance twice led the major leagues in victories; by the end of the decade he was the highest-paid pitcher in baseball. He drove batters to distraction by wearing an outrageously torn and flapping undershirt, until pressure from umpires and irate Chicago Cubs manager Joe McCarthy finally forced Dazzy to adopt the more subdued fashion statement we see in this photograph.

Beans Reardon
National League Umpire, 1926

This man's trademark polka-dot bow tie is in the Baseball Hall of Fame. Here he is in his rookie year, experimenting with a striped prototype. On August 15, 1926, at Ebbets Field in Brooklyn, Beans was faced with the first big test of his career: After some daffily indecisive baserunning by Dazzy Vance, there were suddenly three Dodgers on third base. Despite Vance's culpability in the matter, the umpires had no choice but to declare him the sole rightful possessor of third base.

Reardon, who played bit parts in movies during the off-season, enjoyed gambling at the racetrack with showbiz pals like Al Jolson until the Commissioner of Baseball ordered him to cease his unsavory associations. But Beans refused to give up his favorite pastime, beer drinking. Using his baseball connections, he even managed to acquire a Budweiser distributorship, which he eventually sold to Frank Sinatra for $1 million.

Walter Johnson
1914 Washington Senators

In 1913, the Big Train had his greatest season, winning thirty-six games and pitching twelve shutouts, including a phenomenal fifty-six consecutive scoreless innings. The next year was a letdown for Walter, since he won only twenty-eight games and pitched a measly ten shutouts, but this shy Kansas farm boy had an excellent alibi: He was in love. On June 24, 1914, Walter married Hazel Lee Roberts, the daughter of Nevada Congressman Edward Roberts. The wedding ceremony was performed by the chaplain of the United States Senate.

Patsy Gharrity, Walter Johnson, and Steve O'Neill
1935 Cleveland Indians

The Indians are having a disappointing year, and a gloomy Walter Johnson (center) knows that his days as a major-league manager are numbered. He is flanked by his gloomy coaches, both former big-league catchers. Gharrity (left) was a longtime teammate of Johnson's on the Washington Senators, and O'Neill (right) had spent most of his seventeen-year career with the Indians. The ax finally fell in August, and Johnson's baseball career was over. He was replaced by O'Neill, the man who became rookie pitcher Bob Feller's mentor in 1936.

   Conlon carefully composed this shot to include the wonderfully picturesque baseball debris in the foreground.

Paul Waner
1927 Pittsburgh Pirates

In 1927, Big Poison had his greatest season when he led the National League in hits, RBIs, and batting average and was named the league's Most Valuable Player. He led the Pirates into the World Series where it was their misfortune to be swept by the 1927 New York Yankees. Waner posed for Conlon at Yankee Stadium during this Series.

Paul Waner
1942 Boston Braves

Paul Waner enjoyed a drink now and then. "He had to be a graceful player," said Casey Stengel, "because he could slide without breaking the bottle on his hip." Indeed, in this photograph his eyes are so bloodshot that there is almost an illusion of color. Nevertheless, Waner got his 3000th hit this season and immediately arranged an elaborate blowout for his teammates, family, and friends.

In 1931, Waner swore off alcohol and his batting average fell precipitously: "Jewel Ens was our manager, and he kept inquiring about my off-field activity. He thought I was really burning the candle at both ends when I wasn't burning it at all. Finally he was convinced, and he came to me and told me to have a little fun. Might relax me. Well, I took his advice and started hitting again. Finished the year with something like .321." Actually, he hit .322.

Lou Gehrig
1925 New York Yankees

Why is this rookie smiling?

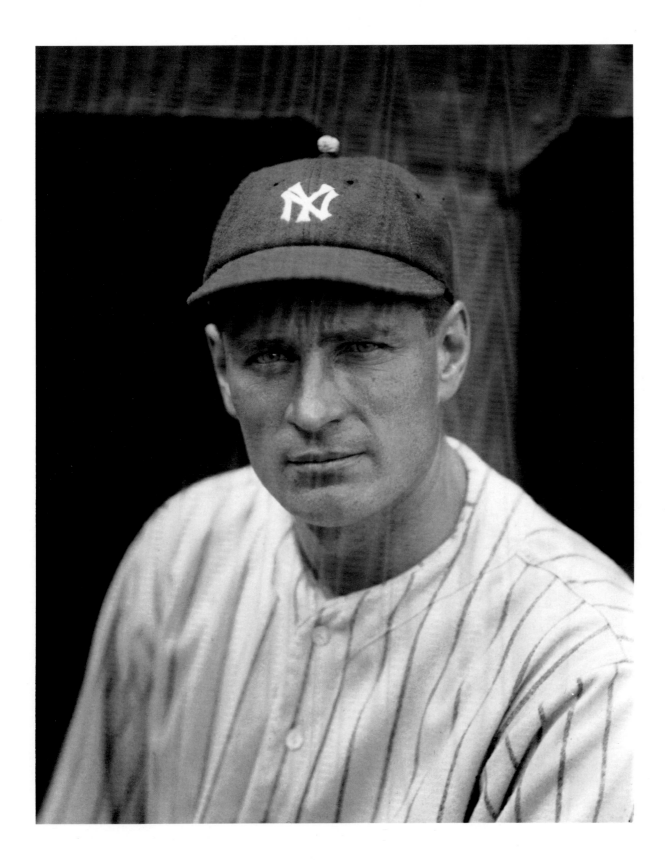

Wally Pipp
1925 New York Yankees

Because this veteran has just taken the day off. Wally Pipp had been the Yankees' regular first baseman for ten years, twice leading the league in home runs, when manager Miller Huggins decided to shake up the lineup of his struggling team. Baseball legend tells us that Wally Pipp had a terrible headache and asked for the day off, but it is more probable that he was benched because he wasn't hitting. In any case, he never played first base for the Yankees again, since Lou Gehrig held down that job for the next fourteen years. Wally Pipp has become a tragicomic actor in a cautionary tale, the victim of cruel fate and a false sense of security, the first person ever to be Wally Pipped.

1913 New York Giants

Conlon never took formal team portraits, but when he came across a rival newspaper photographer setting up a shot, he couldn't pass up the chance. Here is a picture of the National League champions waiting to have their picture taken.

1915 New York Giants

Here is a picture of a last-place team having its picture taken.

← Rogers Hornsby
1924 St. Louis Cardinals

Hornsby was a pretty good second baseman, but he had trouble going back on pop flies. His defensive shortcomings were generally overlooked, as in 1924, when he had the highest batting average of the twentieth century, .424.

Here is the Superba team captain and fan favorite posing for Conlon in the lovely 1913 Brooklyn road uniform. This was the year Daubert won a Chalmers automobile after being named the outstanding player in the National League. He later played first base for the victorious Cincinnati Reds in the infamous 1919 World Series.

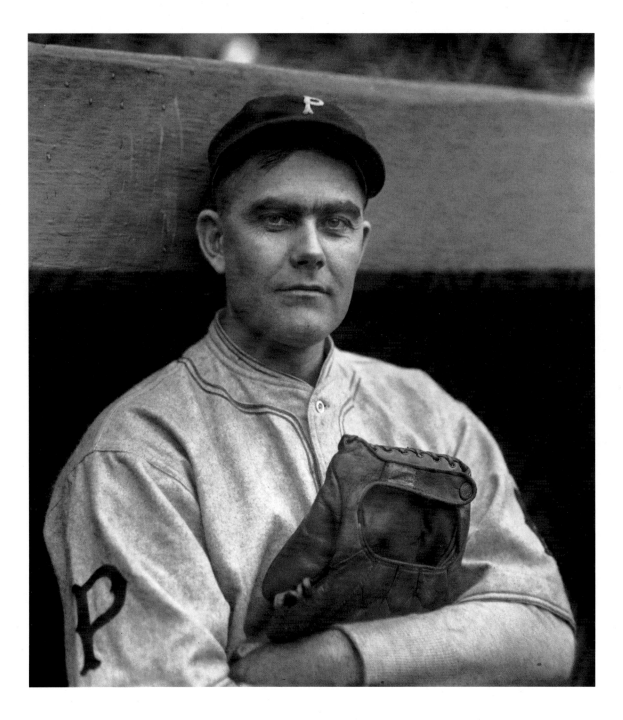

Babe Adams
1924 Pittsburgh Pirates

Sitting in the Pittsburgh dugout before the first game of the 1909 World Series, rookie pitcher Babe Adams joked: "Gee, I wish [Pirate manager Fred] Clarke would pitch me. I'd stand those fellows on their heads. Cobb looks like a sucker to me. And Crawford don't look so hot." Ty Cobb had just won the Triple Crown as he and Wahoo Sam Crawford led the mighty Detroit Tigers to their third straight pennant. Everyone was amused by Adams's absurd boast—everyone, that is, except manager Clarke, who had a hunch. He flipped a shiny new ball to the rookie and said: "You're in, Babe." The stunned Adams proceeded to win three games in the Series, humiliating the Tigers 8–0 in Game Seven to clinch the Pirates' first world championship.

The rest of Babe's long career was solid if unspectacular. He was one of the greatest control pitchers in baseball history, but a sore arm forced him back to the minors in 1917 and 1918. Adams finally appeared in the World Series again when he was a baby-faced forty-three-year-old, pitching one scoreless inning as the Pirates won their second world championship in 1925.

John Bunny
Motion Picture Actor
Shibe Park, Philadelphia, c. 1914

In 1913, this man insured his bulbous face for $50,000. Today he is forgotten, but when Conlon took his photograph at the ballpark, John Bunny was routinely mobbed by his admirers, who numbered in the millions. America's first great screen comic, Bunny was far more famous and beloved than any baseball player alive, and he was earning three times the salary of the great Ty Cobb. When he died in 1915, the 300-pound actor was eulogized around the world, but his fame was instantly eclipsed by a promising young newcomer named Charlie Chaplin.

Lloyd Waner
1929 Pittsburgh Pirates

The Waner brothers were generally ill at ease in front of the camera, but when Conlon asked Lloyd to display the signature on his personalized Louisville Slugger, he shyly, but proudly, complied.

Lon Warneke
1939 St. Louis Cardinals

The proud possessor of the most perfect pompadour in baseball, the Arkansas Hummingbird was a Western Union messenger when he rode his bicycle to the ballpark and announced that he played first base. The Houston Buffaloes didn't need a first baseman, so Lon Warneke became a pitcher. Warneke went on to win 193 games in the National League, and then spent six years as a National League umpire. When his baseball career ended, he became a county judge in Arkansas.

Hans Lobert
1913 Philadelphia Phillies

On his first day in the big leagues, John Bernard Lobert was introduced to John Peter Wagner. The latter, better known as Honus, or Hans, noted the strong resemblance between their noses, and decreed that henceforth Lobert would be known as Hans Number Two.

After the 1913 season, Lobert went on a world tour with John McGraw's New York Giants as they played exhibition games against Charles Comiskey's Chicago White Sox. On this tour McGraw matched Lobert, one of the fastest base runners alive, against a racehorse. Hans and the horse ran a close race around the bases, but umpire Bill Klem declared the horse the winner by a nose. "No horse could beat me by a nose!" protested Lobert. Conlon's photograph suggests that an inquiry was indeed in order.

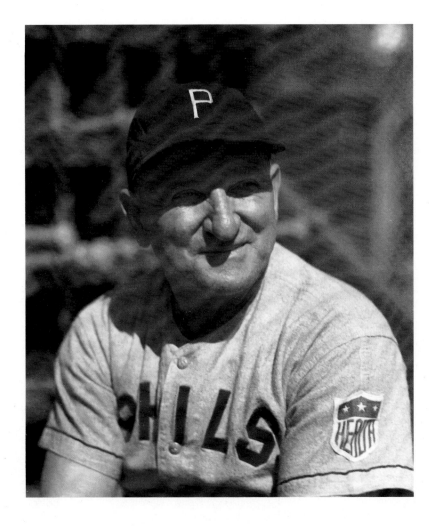

Hans Lobert
1942 Philadelphia Phillies

When Lobert's playing days were over, John McGraw's recommendation won him a prestigious military assignment as the baseball coach at West Point from 1918 until 1925, serving under Douglas MacArthur. By 1942, he was back with the cellar-dwelling Phillies, but even managing the worst team in baseball could not dim Lobert's radiant smile.

Johnny Evers
1904 Chicago Cubs

Evers had a nasty disposition and a high-strung temperament, which caused him to miss most of the 1911 season when he suffered a nervous breakdown. He was generally regarded as the "brainiest man in baseball," yet one thing always puzzled him: "I cannot understand why the umpires don't like me." Perhaps it was because he was the most relentless and obnoxious umpire-baiter in baseball, a man who would protest a rotten call by ostentatiously holding a handkerchief to his nose.

Johnny Evers
1929 Boston Braves

A quarter of a century has elapsed, but the Human Crab has not mellowed. He is now a coach, watching helplessly as the owner and manager of the Boston Braves, Judge Emil Fuchs, guides the team into last place. When Evers managed the Chicago White Sox in 1924, Ed Walsh was one of his coaches: "Whenever we lost, Evers was like a crazy man. He raved and ranted and kicked over chairs and everything else in the clubhouse. I used to listen and say, 'Yeah, Johnny, that's right.' You'd be crazy to disagree with him. And he was rough on umpires too. He had a long chin and when he got in a tiff with an umpire, his chin seemed to be about two feet long."

Fred Merkle
1916 Brooklyn Robins

On September 23, 1908, this man's
life was ruined. During a crucial
game with the Cubs, Johnny Evers
alerted the umpires that Giant rookie Fred Merkle had failed to touch
second base as the winning run
scored. Merkle was called out, the
game was declared a tie, and baseball fans had a scapegoat when the
Giants eventually lost the pennant.
Fred had committed Merkle's Boner,
and he was forever haunted by this
tragic oversight: "I suppose that
when I die, the epitaph on my tomb-
stone will read 'Here lies Bonehead
Merkle.' The tough part of it is that
I can't do things other fellows do
without attracting any attention.
Little slips that would be excused in
any other players are burned into me
by crowds. Of course, I make my
mistakes with the rest, but I have to
do double duty. If any play I'm concerned in goes wrong, I'm the fellow
that gets the blame, no matter where
the thing went off the line. I wish
folks would forget. But they never
will." And they never did.

Bill Wambsganss
1921 Cleveland Indians

On October 10, 1920, this second baseman's life was transformed. With runners on first and second and nobody out, Wambsganss caught a line drive, stepped on second, and tagged the oncoming runner, instantly becoming a hero: He had completed the first and only unassisted triple play in World Series history, and the Indians' 1921 uniforms would read "WORLDS [sic] CHAMPIONS." In later years, Wambsganss complained that this play was the only thing for which he was remembered. He failed to realize that were it not for that one play, he would not be remembered at all.

Enos Slaughter
1938 St. Louis Cardinals

His mad dash around the basepaths, which won the final game of the 1946 World Series for the Cardinals, typified Slaughter's aggressive, supercharged style of play. Conlon photographed this North Carolina country boy during a rare moment of repose in his rookie year.

Smokey Joe Wood
1914 Boston Red Sox

In 1912, Smokey Joe (nicknamed for his "smoking" fastball) had one of the greatest years a pitcher ever had: His record was 34–5 during the regular season, and he won three more games in the World Series. But he hurt his arm in the spring of 1913, and by 1914 Wood was pitching in constant pain. He eventually became an outfielder, rejoining his old Red Sox roommate Tris Speaker on the Cleveland Indians.

← Home Run Baker
1910 Philadelphia Athletics

Frank Baker's nickname seems more than a little ridiculous today, but Conlon's famous photograph captures a classic slugger's swing. Baker's league-leading home run totals (8, 9, 10) are absurdly low when compared with the later totals of Ruth, Foxx, and Greenberg (58, 59, 60), but this photograph demonstrates how dead the ball must have been in the dead-ball era. In 1911, when most batters didn't hit two home runs in a year, Baker hit dramatic home runs in two consecutive World Series games off Rube Marquard and Christy Mathewson, two of the greatest pitchers in baseball history. Home Run Baker's feat was truly phenomenal, and his nickname, well-earned.

John McGraw →
1911 New York Giants

In 1905, John McGraw's Giants showed up for their first World Series in striking black uniforms. Led by Christy Mathewson, who pitched an astonishing three shutouts in the Series, the smartly attired Giants proceeded to demolish the Philadelphia Athletics, four games to one. In 1906, McGraw was not humble about this accomplishment: His team's uniforms now read "WORLD'S CHAMPIONS."

In 1911, the Giants were in their second World Series, and their opponents were once again the Athletics. McGraw was a gambling man who did not wish to tempt fate; therefore black was back. But fate, in the person of Home Run Baker, was not kind to the Giants. This time they lost to the Athletics, four games to two, and black uniforms were forever banished by McGraw.

81

Gabby Hartnett and
Charlie Grimm
1938 Chicago Cubs

Jolly Cholly Grimm (right) was an ambidextrous banjo player who doubled as manager of the Cubs, leading them to the World Series in 1932 and 1935, but he became a radio broadcaster for the Cubs in July of 1938 when he was replaced as manager by catcher Gabby Hartnett. On September 28, 1938, Hartnett hit the "homer in the gloamin'," one of the most dramatic home runs in baseball history: "It was the most sensational thing that ever happened to me," said Hartnett. "I got the kind of feeling you get when the blood rushes to your head and you get dizzy." Gabby's homer took the Cubs to an anticlimactic 1938 World Series, where they were swept by the New York Yankees.

Burleigh Grimes
1938 Brooklyn Dodgers

Joe McCarthy
1938 New York Yankees

Burleigh Grimes (left), the last of the legal spitballers, was nicknamed Ol' Stubblebeard because he never shaved on the day he pitched. His fierce contentiousness made him a Hall of Fame pitcher, but it also made him an unpopular and unsuccessful manager. Here, Burleigh is well shaven and uncharacteristically cordial as he pays his respects to the manager with the highest winning percentage in baseball history. The calm and dignified McCarthy never played in the big leagues, but his teams played in the World Series nine times, and he, too, ended up in the Hall of Fame.

The Dodgers beat the Yankees three games to two in their April 1938 exhibition series. This was the highlight of the year for the Dodgers: They finished in seventh place, while the Yankees, as usual, won the World Series.

Leo Durocher
1925 New York Yankees

This angelic, anonymous rookie was barely visible on the Yankee bench at the end of the 1925 season, batting only twice. Conlon was probably the only person who noticed he was there.

Leo Durocher
1937 St. Louis Cardinals

Leo the Lip, in his last year with the Gas House Gang, was by this point one of the most notorious and colorful ball players in America, impossible for anyone to ignore.

Casey Stengel
1924 Boston Braves

Casey was the batting hero for the New York Giants in the 1923 World Series. His reward? John McGraw traded him to the dismal Boston Braves. This circumstance may explain Stengel's sour expression. The thirty-four-year-old Casey is as yet unrecognizable as the Old Professor he would eventually become in his years as Yankee manager.

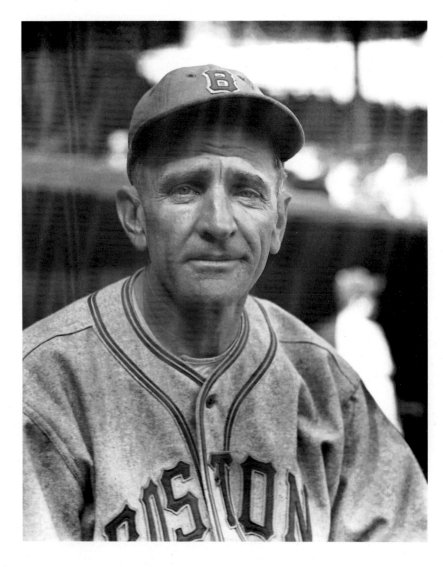

Casey Stengel
1938 Boston Bees

By now we can recognize Casey, but he is not yet a manager destined for the Hall of Fame, particularly since his Boston teams usually finished next to last. The Bees' most notable achievement in 1938 was falling victim to Johnny Vander Meer in the first of his two consecutive no-hitters.

Wahoo Sam Crawford
1917 Detroit Tigers

"Crawford was a tremendous hitter," said Casey Stengel. "Hardly any pitchers which pitched against him is still alive. Half of 'em died of heart attacks." By 1917, his last year in the big leagues, Crawford was no longer lethal at the plate, but he could still put on a good show during batting practice. Americans were going off to fight in World War I, and the Detroit Tigers proclaimed their patriotism by affixing flag patches to their uniforms.

Johnny Vander Meer
1940 Cincinnati Reds

In 1938, Vander Meer pitched back-to-back
no-hitters, an astonishing feat that has
never been duplicated in major-league history. "Someone may tie the record," said
Johnny, "but I don't think anyone will break
it. If someone does, it will be unbelievable."
The next season Vander Meer suffered an
arm injury and was forced to return to the
minor leagues for rehabilitation. In this
photograph, Vander Meer has just returned
to the Reds in order to qualify for the 1940
World Series, where he would pitch three
scoreless innings.

Rick Ferrell
1938 Washington Senators

As a boy, Wes Ferrell refused to play baseball if he couldn't pitch, so his big brother had no choice but to become a catcher. Easygoing Rick Ferrell went on to become the American League catcher in the very first All-Star Game in 1933. When his playing career ended in 1947, Rick had appeared in more games than any other catcher in the history of the American League, and in 1984, he was elected to the Hall of Fame. His brother Wes went on to become the only pitcher to win twenty games in each of his first four big-league seasons.

Wes Ferrell
1929 Cleveland Indians

In 1929, this rookie pitcher threw his glove into the stands after he was removed from a game, and the fans, relishing his discomfort, passed his glove back very, very slowly. "These fans burn me up," he complained. In 1932, he was fined and suspended for refusing to leave a game. "He wasn't well mannered," explained his manager. In 1936, he removed *himself* from a game and was again fined and suspended. After a loss, Wes Ferrell would bang his head against the dugout wall, hit himself in the face with his fist, and tear up his glove with his teeth. "It was all part of an act," he explained in later years. But the young man in this picture is not acting. He is smoldering and ready to explode.

Dizzy Dean
1932 St. Louis Cardinals

Paul Dean
1934 St. Louis Cardinals

Conlon first photographed Dizzy in 1930, before he had ever pitched in a big-league game. In 1932, Dean's rookie season, he became a star by leading the National League in strikeouts, shutouts, and innings pitched. But in June, a petulant Dizzy deserted the team in a salary dispute, vowing that he would leap out of a hotel window rather than play for St. Louis again. He eventually rejoined the Cardinals after a public apology, the episode only adding to Dizzy Dean's box-office value and growing legend.

Unlike his brother Jay Hanna Dean, who gloried in his well-deserved nickname, Dizzy, Paul Dean despised the name Daffy, a newspaper invention. He was quiet and reserved, the temperamental opposite of his brother, but Paul did possess the family fastball. He won nineteen games in both 1934 and 1935, but by 1936 he had thrown his arm out. His brother suffered the same fate a year later.

Babe Ruth
1924 New York Yankees

Before posing for his most famous
Conlon portrait, the Babe considerate-
ly parked his chewing gum on his hat.

Lou Gehrig
1936 New York Yankees

No sooner had the ill-starred Lou Gehrig escaped Babe Ruth's shadow in 1935 than a sensational rookie named Joe DiMaggio joined the Yankees in 1936. An amused Gehrig posed for Conlon during his second MVP season.

Joe Tinker and Frank Chance
1923 Boston Red Sox

Here are two-thirds of the most famous trio in baseball history, the double-play combination of Tinker to Evers to Chance. They set no double-play records, but they sparked the Cubs to four World Series appearances between 1906 and 1910 and inspired an immortal scrap of baseball doggerel. Tinker (left) was an average hitter who, for some reason, "owned" pitcher Christy Mathewson: "The only thing to do is keep them close and try to outguess him," conceded Matty, "but Tinker is a hard man to beat at the game of wits." Chance was the Cubs' manager and Peerless Leader. Conlon captured one of the last meetings between Tinker and Chance, who had not played together in eleven years. Red Sox manager Chance would die the next year.

Johnny Evers
1913 Chicago Cubs

They played side by side on the Cubs, but second baseman Johnny Evers and shortstop Joe Tinker couldn't stand each other: "Sometimes we wouldn't get more than inside the clubhouse after a game when Joe'd bark at me about some play or throw, or I'd yelp at him about something, and we'd drop our gloves and go to it on the floor like a cat and a dog." When they were no longer on speaking terms, the two continued their feud on the field: Tinker would throw to second without even looking, hoping Evers would miss the ball, and Johnny would respond in kind. "Thinking about it now," recalled Evers in his old age, "that sort of thing kept us on our toes—probably kept us in the big leagues."

← Walter Johnson
1910 Washington Senators

In 1910, Johnson won twenty-five games and led the major leagues with a career-high 313 strikeouts. It was the Big Train's first great year, but the editor of the *Spalding Guide* was not impressed: "Johnson, the star pitcher of the Washington club, made a better record than he did in some other years, but there is still room for improvement in his pitching. There is no question that he is one of the most promising pitchers of major-league company, but he lacks that control which is necessary to place him with the leaders in the Base Ball world." Johnson would go on to hit more batters with thrown balls than any other pitcher in major-league history, but somehow he managed to win 416 games.

Moe Berg   →
1935 Boston Red Sox

America's greatest philologist–bullpen catcher–atomic spy, Berg left notes warning his roommates not to touch his stacks of unread foreign-language newspapers: "Don't disturb—they're alive!" The most mysterious man in baseball, he befriended scientists, diplomats, and rookie pitchers with equal ease, but no one really knew Moe Berg.

95

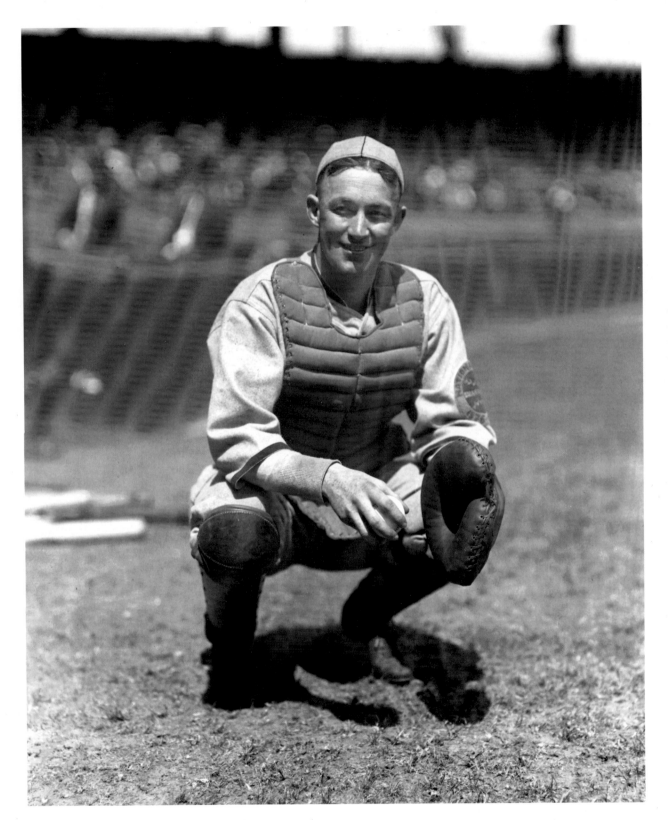

Gabby Hartnett
1925 Chicago Cubs

One day at Wrigley Field in 1931, Gabby signed a baseball for a Cubs fan. Unfortunately, the fan's name was Al Capone, and the horrified Commissioner of Baseball quickly imposed a $5 fine on players caught fraternizing with spectators. Hartnett struck this blithe and beatific pose for Conlon the year he finished second in home runs to Rogers Hornsby. Gabby's little sister, Anna, also a talented ball player, gave exhibitions of her catching prowess at county fairs in New England.

Carl Hubbell
1929 New York Giants

While Hubbell never claimed to have invented the screwball, he was undoubtedly the first pitcher to call it by that name, contributing an invaluable word to the American vocabulary. In 1929, the year of his first and only no-hitter, Hubbell was in his first full season as a Giant starter. He dominated the National League for the next decade, but the American League also fell victim to his screwball: With Gabby Hartnett behind the plate in the 1934 All-Star Game, Hubbell struck out Babe Ruth, Lou Gehrig, Jimmy Foxx, Al Simmons, and Joe Cronin consecutively.

Jimmy Foxx
1929 Philadelphia Athletics

In 1924, Home Run Baker was mightily impressed when he saw sixteen-year-old Jimmy Foxx play baseball: "Baker was so sure that I was going to be a great player that he wrote Connie Mack about me, and Mack bought me for the A's. I reported to Mack in August and when he saw me he said, 'Now I'll be accused of robbing the cradle.'" By 1929, Foxx was the Athletics' regular first baseman. When he retired in 1945, this three-time American League MVP had hit more career home runs than anyone except Babe Ruth.

Babe Ruth
1927 New York Yankees

In the Babe's lifetime, only two batters came close to his 1927 record of sixty home runs: Jimmy Foxx, with fifty-eight in 1932, and Hank Greenberg, with fifty-eight in 1938.

Hack Wilson
1926 Chicago Cubs

"How do I hit 'em? I just go up there with the intention of knocking the ball out of the park and swing!" Hack Wilson's approach to batting was not subtle, but it was undeniably effective: He led the National League in home runs four times, and in 1930 he hit a league-record fifty-six home runs and set the all-time major-league mark with 190 RBIs.

At the top of Wilson's brilliant career, however, everything came crashing down: "I started to drink heavily. I argued with my manager and the rest of the players. I began to spend the winter in taprooms. When spring training rolled around, I was twenty pounds overweight. I couldn't stop drinking. I couldn't hit. That year most experts figured I'd break Ruth's record. But I ended up hitting only thirteen home runs."

Joe Cronin
1932 Washington Senators

How much is your nephew worth? Washington Senators owner Clark Griffith decided that $250,000 sounded about right, so in 1934 he sold Joe Cronin to the Boston Red Sox. Cronin, married to Griffith's niece, was the player-manager of the Senators when they went to the World Series in 1933. He later guided the Red Sox to the 1946 World Series, and in 1959 he became president of the American League.

This picture appeared on Cronin's Big League Chewing Gum baseball card in 1933, but both the cut on his lip and the bandage on his thumb had mysteriously vanished.

← Frenchy Bordagaray
1937 St. Louis Cardinals

When he was fined and suspended for spitting on an umpire, Frenchy demurred: "The penalty is a little more than I expectorated." Bordagaray scandalized the baseball world in 1936 by growing a moustache, and he was the percussionist for Pepper Martin's Musical Mudcats in the last days of the Gas House Gang: "I learned how to play the washboard in three easy lessons in the clubhouse at St. Petersburg. We used to drive [Cardinal manager] Frankie Frisch nuts." His exasperated teammate Joe Medwick was driven to inquire: "What the hell are we running, a ball club or a musical comedy?" But seriously, folks, Frenchy could hit: He was the leading pinch hitter in the National League in 1938, when he batted .465.

Cy Rigler →
National League Umpire, 1911

During his first month as a major-league umpire in 1906, Rigler declared: "It is a mistake to suppose that I am in the game as a fighter. I am not seeking for trouble and hope that none will ever come in any game in which I am the umpire." Few dared challenge this intimidating ex-football player, but when trouble did come, Rigler was ready to rumble. Buck Herzog and Frankie Frisch were among the disputants he whacked with his mask during his thirty-year career.

The wooden grandstand of the Polo Grounds burned down after the second game of the 1911 season, and the Giants were forced to relocate to tiny Hilltop Park, the home of the New York Highlanders. But as this photograph reveals, the Giants returned to the Polo Grounds while construction of their new steel-and-concrete grandstand was still far from complete. The rush job was finished just in time for the 1911 World Series.

Wally Schang
1917 Philadelphia Athletics

One of the most valuable players of his time, this rifle-armed catcher played in the World Series for the A's in 1913 and 1914, for the Red Sox in 1918, and for the Yankees in 1921, 1922, and 1923. The baseball world took note when the eminent Mr. Schang decided to shave before the 1918 season, and he has gone down in history as the last "moustachioed" man of the dead-ball era.

John Henry
1918 Boston Braves

In 1917, catcher John Henry of the Washington Senators urged his teammates to join the Base Ball Players' Fraternity in a strike against the major leagues. American League president Ban Johnson promised to crush the fledgling union: "We propose to lay a strong hand on Henry and others like him." Henry's reply was less than diplomatic: "Johnson has no power to ride me out of the American League. He is trying to make me the goat. Just because I have been a good fellow, friendly with the magnates, and liked by my mates, he is picking on me. Well, let him. Johnson is crazy for power." Needless to say, the revolt quickly fizzled, and Henry was humiliated: The "rattle-brained agitator" and "disturber" was forced to accept a $1200 reduction in his annual salary of $4600. In 1918, Henry ended his career in the National League, and only Charles M. Conlon took note of the shell-shocked pariah's new moustache.

In the spring of 1972, Reggie Jackson brought the moustache back to baseball—and major-league players finally went out on strike.

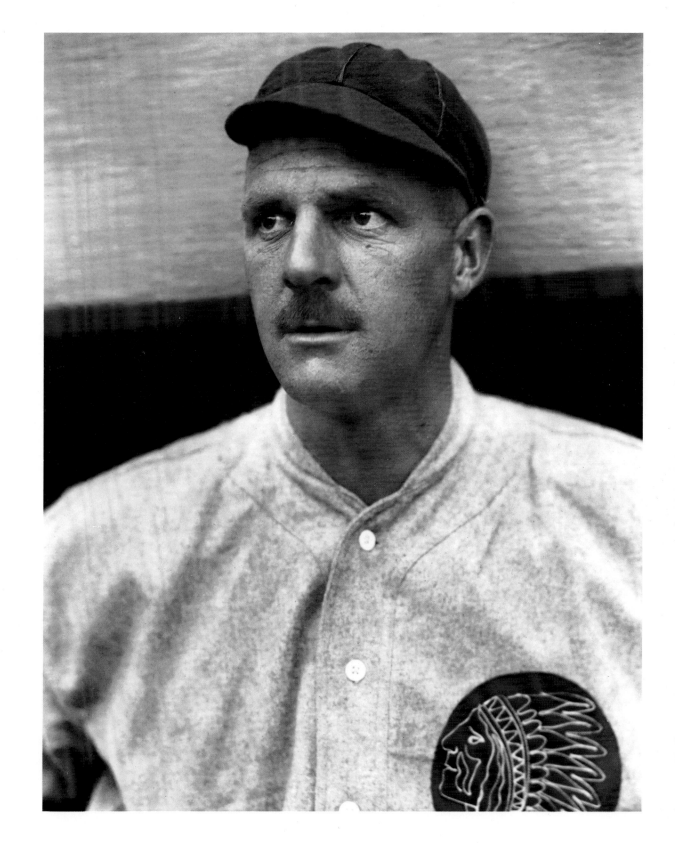

Luke Sewell
1921 Cleveland Indians

Luke snuck into the big leagues for only three games at the end of the 1921 season, but the observant Conlon spotted the new face. Sewell enrolled at the University of Alabama as a fifteen-year-old and played quarterback for the Crimson Tide in 1920. He later managed the St. Louis Browns to their one and only American League pennant in 1944. As manager of the Cincinnati Reds in the early 1950s, he made a visionary innovation: He ordered the groundskeepers to drag the infield midway through each game, simultaneously smoothing the playing surface and increasing concession sales during this extended break in the action.

Miller Huggins
1927 New York Yankees

"It wasn't an easy task to handle such monkeys as we had on the Yankees," recalled third baseman Joe Dugan. "And that big Bambino, Ruth—I mean, he was probably enough for three managers." Outfielder Bob Meusel agreed: "Those Yankees of the twenties were pretty rough outfits. It was Hug's place to tell us when we got out of hand." In this famous Conlon portrait, the Yankee manager's face shows the strain of trying—and failing—to tame Babe Ruth and the other members of Murderers' Row.

Throughout his decades-long career, Conlon never took extreme close-ups of his subjects' faces—except for the afternoon when he took mug shots of Murderers' Row, the fabled starting lineup of the 1927 New York Yankees, featured on the following pages.

107

Earle Combs
1927 New York Yankees

"I have never gone in much for liquor. Some of the boys on those Huggins clubs could not understand how a Kentuckian did not drink. One of them came to me in 1925 and said, 'Combs, if you expect to stay on this club, you had better learn to drink.'" Despite threats and peer pressure, the Yankees' lead-off hitter remained a lifelong teetotaler, nonsmoker, and devoted Bible reader. A weak-armed center fielder, Combs had the misfortune of playing between Babe Ruth and Bob Meusel, the men with the best throwing arms in baseball, but the Kentucky Colonel made up for his defensive shortcomings with a .325 career batting average.

Mark Koenig
1927 New York Yankees

Koenig was a light-hitting shortstop who led the league in errors in 1927, but he was also the man who batted just before Ruth and Gehrig in the lineup of Murderers' Row. He hit .500 in the 1927 World Series, leading all batters.

In 1932, Koenig helped the Chicago Cubs win the pennant, whereupon he became indirectly responsible for one of the most famous moments in baseball history. The Yankees felt that their ex-teammate had been poorly treated by the Cubs when they voted him only a half share of the World Series money. The two teams' increasingly acrimonious exchanges of insults and hand gestures finally culminated in Babe Ruth's called shot, the home run he definitely did or did not predict in pantomime.

Babe Ruth
1927 New York Yankees

"Here you may meet baseball's greatest slugger face to face. Babe Ruth, the Superman of Swat—most picturesque of ball players, the greatest slugger who ever lived." This caption appeared with Conlon's photograph when it was first published in the September 1927 issue of *Baseball Magazine*.

When this most picturesque of ball players hit sixty home runs in 1927, he easily surpassed the next-highest home run total in the American League, the fifty-six home runs hit collectively by the Philadelphia Athletics.

Pat Collins
1927 New York Yankees

Babe Ruth called everybody Kid because he had difficulty remembering names, but for teammates he would make exceptions. Here is the man Ruth called Horse Nose. Collins was a substitute catcher throughout his career, but in 1927 he played in more games than any other Yankee catcher and contributed seven home runs to the Yankees' league-leading total of 158.

Ben Paschal
1927 New York Yankees

Babe Ruth suffered a "bilious attack" on Opening Day in 1927. It was something he ate, according to Yankee manager Miller Huggins, so Ben Paschal was sent in to pinch-hit. Paschal was accustomed to substituting for the Babe, since he had replaced Ruth for much of the 1925 season when the slugger had been similarly indisposed.

Paschal had batted .360 then, but when the best player in baseball returned, Ben was back on the bench. A reserve outfielder who played in only 364 major-league games, Paschal was entitled to a mug shot as an auxiliary member of Murderers' Row.

← Jack Graney
1911 Cleveland Naps

Fun-loving Graney had a bull terrier named Larry who traveled with the Naps as their mascot and put on crowd-pleasing acrobatic exhibitions before their games. During a game in Washington in 1914, Larry retrieved a foul ball. Unfortunately, even human fans had to give foul balls back in those days, and when Larry refused to surrender the ball to umpire Big Bill Dinneen, the dog was banished from the Washington ballpark by order of American League president Ban Johnson.

Graney was the first player to wear a number on his uniform, the first ex-athlete to become a professional broadcaster, and the first major leaguer to bat against rookie pitcher Babe Ruth (he singled).

Woodrow Wilson →
Baker Bowl, Philadelphia
October 9, 1915

When Jack Graney and his Cleveland teammates visited the White House, the president of the United States had only one question: "Where's Larry? I've got to meet that extraordinary dog!" The White House doorman was ordered to produce the Naps' mascot, whereupon Larry gave a command performance for Woodrow Wilson.

Conlon photographed the first president ever to attend a World Series when Woodrow Wilson threw out the first ball before Game Two of the 1915 World Series between the Phillies and Red Sox. Wilson was also the first president to arrive late for a World Series game, delaying the start of the contest by several minutes. This was the first public appearance of Wilson and his fiancée, Mrs. Edith Bolling Galt. Their engagement had been announced three days previously.

← Lefty Grove
1925 Philadelphia Athletics

When the Martinsville team of the Blue Ridge League needed a new outfield fence in 1920, they sold Lefty Grove, their most valuable asset, to Jack Dunn and the Baltimore Orioles for $3500. Five years later, Dunn sold him to Connie Mack and the A's for $100,600. The rookie glared at everyone as menacingly as he glared at Conlon: "I was suspicious of everybody. And I guess I was scared of big cities. My attitude was the best defense I could think of. I figured that if I scared people away, they wouldn't steal my money and my watch." Even his own teammates were uneasy around Grove, who was known to tear up the locker room after a loss.

Lefty Grove →
1937 Boston Red Sox

In 1937, Charles M. Conlon told *The Sporting News*: "In photographing ball players, you run into a lot of difficulties, mainly because they are so superstitious. Lefty Grove still is one of the most persistent believers in that sort of thing. If you don't believe me, try to get him to pose his pitching hand holding the ball. Nobody has ever got that picture, and I guess nobody ever will. Lefty thinks this picture would reveal the secret of his skill. He always tells you, 'There is nothing good-looking about my hand.'"

In 1941, Grove retired with exactly 300 victories, the secret of his pitching skill intact.

119

Hank Greenberg
1933 Detroit Tigers

In 1929, eighteen-year-old first baseman Hank Greenberg was offered a contract by his hometown team, the Yankees. He declined, noting that they already had a first baseman named Gehrig, who never missed a game. In 1933, rookie Greenberg returned triumphantly to the Bronx as the regular first baseman of the Detroit Tigers.

Hank Greenberg
1940 Detroit Tigers

Greenberg won his second Most Valuable Player award in 1940, leading the Tigers to the World Series. He missed the next four and a half seasons while serving in World War II, but he returned in mid-1945, again leading the Tigers to the World Series with a pennant-winning grand-slam home run on the final day of the season.

Chief Meyers
1909 New York Giants

When the 1910 season ended, Chief Meyers and Christy Mathewson appeared together in a vaudeville act entitled "Curves," in which Matty demonstrated his famous "fadeaway" pitch and Chief portrayed his catcher. The two then demonstrated their inconsiderable acting talents in a dramatic sketch that made this college-educated Native American cringe: A courageous cowboy, played by Mathewson, rescued a fair maiden from the clutches of a bloodthirsty savage, played by Meyers. Mercifully, the sketch flopped when it was greeted by laughter, much to Matty's consternation.

George Moriarty →
1910 Detroit Tigers

Moriarty was a journalist, inventor, songwriter, and the self-proclaimed "poet laureate of baseball," whose magnum opus was entitled "Don't Die on Third." He became an American League umpire in 1917, quit to succeed his old teammate Ty Cobb as manager of the Tigers in 1927, and then became an umpire again in 1929. Moriarty's most memorable day at the ballpark came on Memorial Day in 1932, when he offered to fight the entire Chicago White Sox team, one man at a time. The White Sox misunderstood, and jumped the pugnacious umpire en masse. He was hospitalized with head injuries and a broken hand, but only briefly.

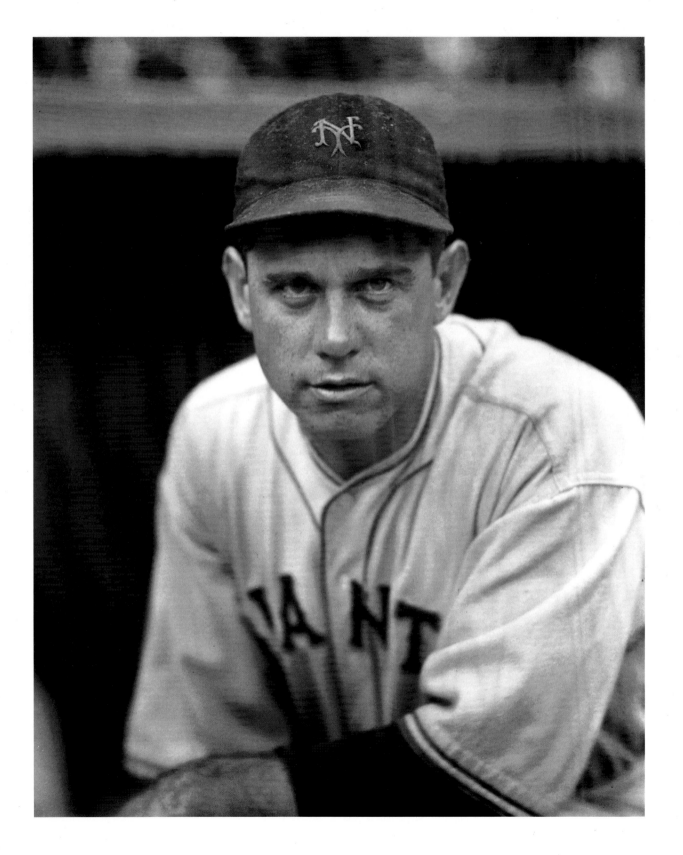

Bill Terry
1934 New York Giants

Terry became the last .400 hitter in the National League when he batted .401 in 1930. He succeeded John McGraw as Giant manager in 1932 and led the team to a world championship in 1933. In January 1934, after Terry predicted that the Giants would again win the pennant, a sportswriter asked: "Do you fear Brooklyn?" The arrogant and tactless Terry responded with a sarcastic question that would torpedo his team's pennant hopes and resound in baseball history: "Is Brooklyn still in the league?" The sixth-place Dodgers avenged this insult by gleefully defeating the Giants in the last two games of the 1934 season, thus enabling the St. Louis Cardinals to beat out Terry's team for the pennant by exactly two games.

John McGraw
1905 New York Giants

In the 1890s, Muggsy McGraw was a brilliant third baseman for the Baltimore Orioles. He made an art form out of tripping base runners while the umpire wasn't looking, but he also perfected the hit-and-run play with Oriole teammate Wee Willie Keeler. Here the Giant manager poses as a first baseman, although he played only one game at the position during his entire sixteen-year career, and he wears his 1904 uniform with his 1905 hat, typical in an era when uniforms were not necessarily uniform. The 1905 Giants always remained John McGraw's favorites, not only because they were his first world champions, but because he considered them the smartest of all his teams.

1904 New York Giants

Here is the only team that ever refused to play in the World Series. Actually, the players very much wanted to play in the Series, but manager John McGraw and team owner John T. Brush were feuding with Ban Johnson and the four-year-old American League: "There is nothing in the constitution or playing rules of the National League which requires its victorious club to submit its championship honors to a contest with a victorious club in a minor league," declared the arrogant Giant owner. There followed an immediate hail of criticism from the fans and the press, accusing McGraw and Brush of cowardice, and bitter complaints from the Giant players, who had been concerned about being deprived of a large postseason paycheck. The 1905 World Series went on as scheduled.

Jimmy Archer
c. 1913 Chicago Cubs

"Here is a hand with a history. The first and fourth fingers look like the wreck of the Hesperus. The little finger curves like a barrel hoop. Jimmy couldn't straighten it out to save his life but it didn't bother him any as he said 'the ball fitted well into the curve.' The first finger is grown to about two sizes owing to the fact that both joints have been repeatedly broken. That is some finger. The other two fingers might not do over well for a violin player, but they are quite straight and normal for a catcher. Not saying that they have not met with their mishaps. Jimmy broke every finger of this hand. But the fractures didn't result in such odd shoots and angles as were assumed by the other fingers in the healing process."

This description of Archer's hand was illustrated by Conlon's photograph in the October 1917 issue of *Baseball Magazine*. Editor F. C. Lane collaborated with Conlon again the next year on a bizarre article entitled "Inside Dope from a Ball Player's Hands." The illustrations consisted entirely of close-ups of famous players' hands. Sadly, none of these twenty-five negatives now exist.

Wes Ferrell
1938 Washington Senators

In December 1938, Charles M. Conlon made a proposal to *The Sporting News*: "It seems to me that a discussion among your readers on 'Who is the handsomest player in the majors?' might prove interesting. Quite a number of the boys would qualify in Hollywood if good looks were the only requirement." A poll was conducted and the winner was . . . Wes Ferrell. An autographed photo of Wes was awarded to the woman who best explained her choice: "His head is well shaped; his eyes are neither too far apart, nor too close together; his nose is in the middle of his face, where it belongs, not off to one side; and most important of all, his ears are close to his head. No matter how you look at him, he's handsome."

The seventy-year-old Conlon had a simpler explanation: "It's his hair. The girls like his marcel."

Bill Lee
1936 Chicago Cubs

The first runner-up in Conlon's beauty contest was Bill Lee, the Cubs' ace pitcher who led the majors in wins and shutouts in 1938. He was a Plaquemine, Louisiana, native who had imbibed the traditions of the bayou: "You might call it super-stitious when I insist upon putting down my glove a cer-tain way and demanding that no one touch it. And I always take four, and only four, warm-up pitches at the start of an inning and I won't pose for a picture on the day I'm going to pitch."

Here Conlon captures an amazing simulation of a warm-up pitch, performed by Bill Lee and his Lucky Glove.

Napoleon Lajoie
1909 Cleveland Naps

In 1909, Lajoie was the highest-paid player in baseball, managing a team named in his honor. "Jumpin' Jehosophat, how he does sock 'em!" raved *The Sporting News*. "Infielders frequently are bowled over like tenpins by his terrific liners, and even the outfielders have difficulty handling them." After a quarter-century of retirement, Lajoie recalled those days wistfully: "If I could make one wish that would come true, I'd wish that the boys I was playing with in 1908 could operate on that jack-rabbit ball they're throwing today, just for one season. My biggest regret is that I never had an opportunity to take a few swipes at it. When I think of how hard we used to hit the dead ball, I begin to wonder why some of these modern-day pitchers haven't been killed."

George Stovall
1914 Kansas City Packers

On August 3, 1907, in a Philadelphia hotel dining room, Cleveland first baseman George Stovall called Napoleon Lajoie a vile name, and the Naps' manager fined him $50. Stovall repeated his insult and suggested that Lajoie double the fine. "All right, I'll make it $100," replied the agreeable Lajoie. "Does that go?" inquired Stovall. "You can bet it does!" said Lajoie, at which point Stovall picked up a heavy oak chair and attempted to crush his manager's skull. Only the quick reflexes of Cleveland pitcher Dusty Rhoads, who deflected the chair, prevented a serious injury. Lajoie suffered a glancing blow to the head, and the chair splintered on the floor. "We did have a little mite of a disagreement," recalled Stovall forty years later, "but it never amounted to as much as they said. Guess we'd be good friends now if we met."

Because of such incendiary behavior, Stovall became known as Firebrand and the Human Torch. Incredibly, he became the Naps' manager in 1911 and then managed the St. Louis Browns in 1912 and 1913. He temporarily relinquished the latter position after drenching an umpire with tobacco juice. In 1914, Stovall became the first major-league player to jump to the outlaw Federal League: "Someone had to be first," he explained, "and it might as well be I." Kansas City manager Stovall posed for Conlon in the first year of the league's two-year existence; this is the only Conlon Federal League portrait that survives as a negative.

← Benny Bengough
1932 St. Louis Browns

"A good catcher should be able to tell whether he can catch a foul ball by the crack of the bat and the first flash he gets of the ball as he turns around," said Benny Bengough, the man who actually described foul balls as "the spice of life." Here he rapturously removes his catcher's mask for Conlon's camera, a phantom pop foul illuminating his eyes. In 1917, Benny was a lowly minor-league bullpen catcher when his mother complained that her boy never got a chance to play. The manager got the message and Bengough's baseball career got its start. He eventually became a back-up catcher for the greatest team in baseball history, the 1927 New York Yankees.

In 1933, this picture appeared on card #1 of the first baseball bubble-gum card set ever issued. Today, that Benny Bengough card is an exceedingly rare and costly collectible.

Babe Ruth and Lou Gehrig →
1926 New York Yankees

Conlon took thousands of photographs of players simply warming up on the sidelines, pictures that satisfied the curiosity of baseball fans in the pre-television era who wanted to see what their heroes looked like in their everyday environment. These scenes seem all the more unreal to us today precisely because they were once so commonplace. Here is a representative example: two guys playing catch—one named Ruth, one named Gehrig.

Ex-pitcher Babe Ruth superstitiously insisted on warming up with a Yankee catcher before each game. From 1920 to 1924, his partner was Fred Hofmann. From 1925 to 1930, his partner was Benny Bengough.

Fred Hofmann
1922 New York Yankees

Hofmann was a jovial benchwarmer, always prepared to party. He thus fulfilled all of the qualifications necessary to become Babe Ruth's roommate, a position he occupied for three years. Although Hofmann's accepted nickname was Bootnose, his roomie preferred the more elemental Crooked Nose. Fred was naturally along for the ride when Ruth was in an auto accident and reported killed in 1920. His greatest thrill in baseball came when he drew a base on balls in the 1923 World Series.

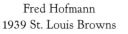

Fred Hofmann
1939 St. Louis Browns

Hofmann was a highly knowledge-
able baseball man. In 1922, and
again in 1928, he traveled to Japan
to give baseball exhibitions that
helped popularize the sport in that
country. Fred was a coach for the
St. Louis Browns when they played
in their only World Series in 1944,
and he stayed with the team when
they moved to Baltimore in 1954.
He scouted future Hall of Famer
Brooks Robinson and later discovered and signed future Oriole great
Boog Powell.

Honus Wagner
1914 Pittsburgh Pirates

"Hans is awkward. His best friends admit that. There's no airy, fairy grace about him. When he moves from his favorite position to stop a hot one, it's like a standing army mobilizing for a night march or a naval monitor getting under way. His tread is a cross between that of the elephant and rhinoceros. In reaching for the leather, his arms look like cotton hooks and move about as gracefully as steam cranes. Hans is built along the lines of a threshing machine. But—he gets there just the same. It must be conceded that there are mighty few drives that get by him. And the average fan, watching the speed and certainty with which Hans goes after the grassers and yanks down the soarers, forgets the shortstop's seeming clumsiness and thinks of him rather as the 'Flying Dutchman.'" (*The Sporting News*, March 3, 1906)

Honus Wagner
1936 Pittsburgh Pirates

"Not so long ago, a friend asked me when I was going to give up the game. 'Never,' I told him, and I meant it. I'll never want to quit, and I'll be tagging around with ball players as long as I can walk. I am right where I want to be—as a coach with the Pirates. This is the team I played with for so many years, and I get a real kick out of being on deck in the monkey suit every day, taking my turn at batting them to the boys and going out to the coaching line." Honus finally hung up his spikes after the 1951 season, at the age of seventy-seven. He lived long enough to see an enormous statue of himself dedicated by the city of Pittsburgh in 1955.

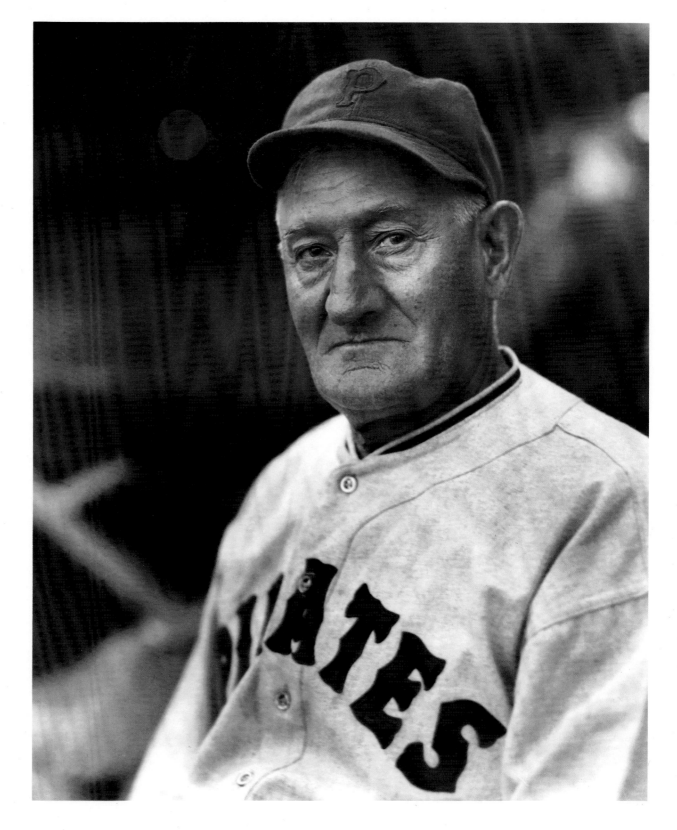

Honus Wagner
1910 Pittsburgh Pirates

"I have sometimes wished I could have batted against the lively ball," said Honus in the 1930s. "In my day, the ball was pretty dead and you had to wallop it to make it go. A home run was something to get you a headline all the way across the top of the page in the newspapers, and always brought out an extra 500 fans the next day. Of course, I don't know if I would have hit any better against the lively ball."

In 1927, when asked what he thought Honus Wagner could have done with the lively ball, Ring Lardner replied simply: "He couldn't have hit it much farther than he hit the old one." In this photograph, Wagner displays the slashing power that so impressed his contemporaries. His Pirate teammates are obviously impressed, but then so were his opponents: "When Pittsburgh had infield or batting practice, we just sat on the bench to watch Wagner's every move," said New York Giant catcher Chief Meyers. "He was the best."

Tommy Leach
1910 Pittsburgh Pirates

Conlon took several photographs during batting practice this day at Washington Park in Brooklyn. It is now a few moments later, and a former home-run king has stepped in to take his cuts. True, he hit only six home runs in 1902 (the lowest league-leading total of this century), and all of them were hit inside the park, but this was still quite an accomplishment for Tommy the Wee, a man dismissed from a tryout in 1898 with these words: "We don't play midgets on the Giants."

Washington Park was a terrible place to play baseball. Brooklyn lived in dread of fire in the wooden stands, and the conditions were intolerable for players and spectators alike: "If any breeze did get a notion to stir," wrote John B. Foster, "it was choked to death by the big chimney on the other side of Third Avenue, which belched forth smoke and cinders all of the afternoon. Once the park warmed up well, it so remained. Fans went to the field prepared to swim in perspiration, and usually they did." The opening of modern Ebbets Field in 1913 was truly a breath of fresh air for baseball in Brooklyn.

← Wilbert Robinson, John McGraw, and Christy Mathewson 1912 New York Giants

Beginning in 1910, Charles M. Conlon covered the World Series as a photojournalist for thirty years. He photographed the crowd outside the ballpark and the paying customers within. He photographed all of the pregame activities: the march of the teams from the clubhouse; the traditional handshakes between managers, starting pitchers, and mascots; the postseason award presentations; the first-ball ceremony. When the game began, he took action shots of every exciting play. Today, virtually all of these negatives are lost.

The men in this photograph are not posing. Pitching coach Robinson (left), manager McGraw (center), and pitcher Mathewson (right) are at brand-new Fenway Park in Boston, anxiously awaiting the start of a game during one of the most nerve-racking World Series ever played. A vendor can be seen hawking souvenir pennants behind the dugout. The Giants would lose the eighth and deciding game to the Red Sox at Fenway Park following an infamous muffed fly ball by Fred Snodgrass and a disastrous mental error by Christy Mathewson, who called for catcher Chief Meyers to take a foul pop-up he could not reach.

Zack Wheat
1912 Brooklyn Superbas

Zack and Daisy Wheat were married in 1912, eight days after they had met at Redland Field in Cincinnati. Wheat was the highest-paid Superba that year, earning the grand sum of $3300, but he was worth it because he put fans in the box seats. Brooklyn florist and baseball enthusiast W. C. Martin became overly excited one day in 1915 when Wheat hit a game-tying home run in the bottom of the ninth. Mr. Martin complained of chest pains but survived into extra innings, long enough to see Wheat knock in the winning run in the eleventh. "Mr. Martin gave a great yell of joy, then sank back quietly in his seat," reported *The Sporting News*. Zack Wheat had killed his first fan.

Wahoo Sam Crawford
1912 Detroit Tigers

Conlon intended to document Crawford's batting grip in this photograph, but he also captured Wahoo Sam's characteristically peevish expression. Crawford played a pivotal role in the bizarre incident that occurred here at Hilltop Park on May 15, 1912. A fan in the stands persisted in taunting Ty Cobb, using highly charged racist language. When Crawford asked Cobb if he was going to tolerate such abuse, Ty jumped into the stands and attacked the fan. It turned out that the heckler was missing one hand entirely and had only two fingers on the other, but Ty Cobb beat him up all the same. American League president Ban Johnson witnessed the incident and suspended Cobb, whereupon the Tigers went on a one-day strike to protest the decision. On May 18, 1912, the Philadelphia Athletics trounced a ragtag collection of college and semipro ball players who were Detroit Tigers for a day. The final score was 24–2.

← Hughie Jennings
1909 Detroit Tigers

An overflow crowd lines the outfield fence at Hilltop Park as manager Hughie Jennings exhorts his Tigers to capture their third straight American League pennant. The runner taking his lead off third base on the far right is, not surprisingly, Wahoo Sam Crawford, the man who set the all-time major-league record for triples.

Jennings, a Cornell graduate, was a practicing attorney in the off-season. When he was the captain of the champion Baltimore Orioles in the 1890s, his teammates included Wee Willie Keeler, John McGraw, Wilbert Robinson, and Kid Gleason.

← Hughie Jennings
1910 Detroit Tigers

Conlon took a famous series of photographs of Jennings, whose distinctive body language was accompanied by an unforgettable ear-splitting scream. "I used to say, 'That's the way!' Then I found that it was too dull and tiresome. I wanted something with snap and go to it. So I changed it to 'That's the way-ah!' From this I changed it to just 'The way-ah!' Finally I found I was just yelling 'Ee-yaah!'"

Christy Mathewson: "Hughie Jennings emits his famous 'Ee-yaah!' and the third baseman creeps in, expecting Cobb to bunt with a man on first base and no one out. The hitter pushes the ball on a line past the third baseman. The next time Jennings shrieks his famous war-cry, it has a different intonation, and the batter bunts."

Hughie Jennings
1912 Detroit Tigers

On March 9, 1912, this grim news was reported to the baseball world: "Manager Hughie Jennings, of the Detroit team, will not be able to coach after the fashion that has made him famous when the American League season opens next month, unless something akin to a miracle happens. Five months have passed since Jennings was injured in an auto smash-up, and he still is crippled. He can't twist his wrist enough to get his fingers to his lips to whistle, and he will have trouble picking grass. He can't kick and prance, for one leg is so weak he has to nurse it carefully. If Jennings has not been able to recover more than this in five months there is not much chance that he will in four weeks more. There is a fear that his injuries may be permanent."

But sometimes miracles happen. Hughie recovered to kick and prance again that season.

Tris Speaker
1916 Cleveland Indians

Speaker was the greatest center fielder of his generation, yet the Red Sox sold him to Cleveland just before Opening Day in 1916 when he refused to accept a fifty percent pay cut. In a famous portrait, the Gray Eagle peers intently at Conlon's lens, his icy gaze betraying the bitterness he felt at leaving Boston, the city where he had become an institution. Tris responded to this shattering development by having one of his best years for his new team. He batted .386 in 1916 to lead the American League in hitting, thus depriving Ty Cobb of the chance to win a mind-boggling thirteen consecutive batting titles. Between 1907 and 1919, only Speaker was able to surpass Cobb at the plate.

Tris Speaker
1928 Philadelphia Athletics

"Tris Speaker resents being joshed about his age. He says that just so long as he continues to go at top speed it really does not matter how much the fans 'ride' him because his hair is gray, but that it hurts him when he is going bad. Speaker refuses to divulge his exact age, but declares that he has been gray since he was seventeen years of age and that he is not yet thirty. Few fans will believe that Tris is as young as he would like people to believe, but, after all, what does it matter? He is playing the greatest game of his career, and until he starts to slip the fans in Cleveland will not worry about his gray hair."

The justifiably sensitive Speaker was indeed only twenty-eight years old when this item appeared in *The Sporting News* in 1916. By 1928, however, he was in his twenty-second and last major-league season, his playing skills having finally caught up with his hair.

145

Tony Lazzeri
1929 New York Yankees

On October 10, 1926, in the seventh inning of the seventh game of the World Series, St. Louis Cardinals pitcher Grover Cleveland Alexander struck out Tony Lazzeri with the bases loaded. It was one of the most dramatic moments in World Series history. In 1930, Lazzeri good-naturedly called that strikeout his greatest thrill in baseball, but by 1945, the year before his death, he was tired of hearing about it: "Funny thing, but nobody seems to remember much about my ball playing except that strikeout. There isn't a night goes by but what some guy leans across the bar, or comes up behind me at a table in this joint, and brings up the old question. Never a night. All they want to talk about is that damn time I struck out."

Grover Cleveland Alexander
1917 Philadelphia Phillies

When he fell on hard times after his retirement from baseball, Alexander reenacted his legendary strikeout for the customers of a Times Square freak show. At the heart of the legend was the allegation that Alexander was nursing a brutal hangover when he came in from the bullpen to strike out Lazzeri, but the pitcher always denied that he had been out drinking the night before: "I don't want to spoil anyone's story, but I was cold sober that night. There were plenty of other nights, before and since, that I wasn't, but that night I was as sober as a judge should be." Cardinal manager Rogers Hornsby concurred, adding indignantly: "I would be a hell of a manager if I put a drunken pitcher in to save the last game of a World Series, wouldn't I?"

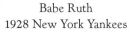

Babe Ruth
1928 New York Yankees

Ruth could never quite bring himself to say that he had actually called his shot against Charlie Root in the 1932 World Series. Here is his typically evasive 1936 version, surreally fractured by a Detroit sportswriter who rendered the Babe's expletives suitable for public consumption: "Every time I went to bat the Cubs on the bench would yell, 'Oogly googly.' It's all part of the game, but that particular inning when I went to bat, there was a whole chorus of oogly googlies. The first pitch was a pretty good strike and I didn't kick, but the second was outside and I turned around to beef about it. As I did, Gabby Hartnett said, 'Oogly googly.' That kinda burned me and I said, 'All right you bums, I'm going to knock this one a mile.' I guess I pointed, too. The next pitch was a fast one and I got a hold of it. Before I started to first base I turned to Gabby Hartnett and said, right back to him, 'Oogly googly.' It was the first time I ever knew him not to have an answer. He didn't say a word."

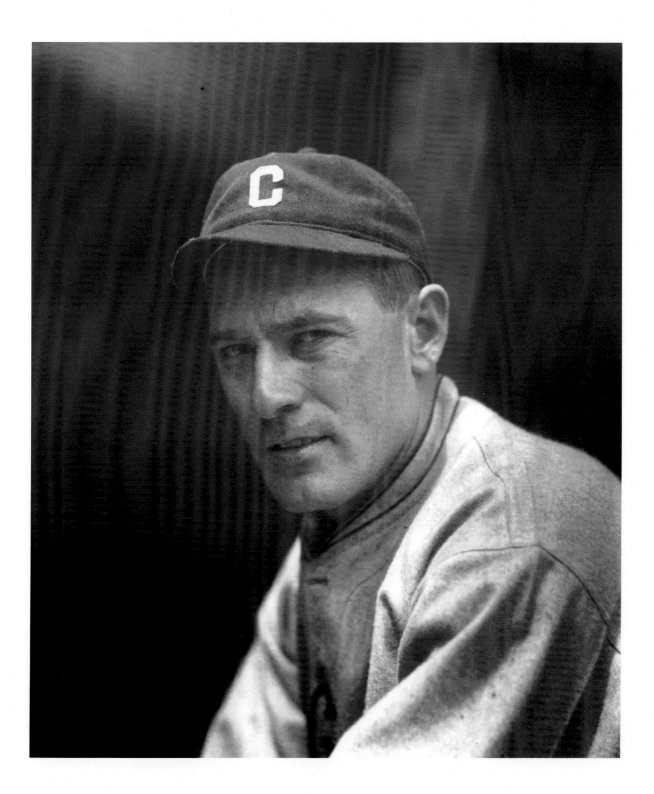

Charlie Root
1926 Chicago Cubs

Root always denied that Ruth had called his shot: "Baloney. If he had pointed to the stands, he'd have gone down on his fanny. I'd have loosened him up. Nobody facing me would have gotten away with that." This notorious headhunter wasn't bluffing: A distressed Brooklyn sportswriter once complained that Charlie seemed to be throwing at Dodger hitters "for the sheer fun of it," and Cubs manager Charlie Grimm was so impressed by Root's jaw-thrusting belligerence that he dubbed him Chinski. Offered the chance to play himself in *The Babe Ruth Story* (the worst baseball movie ever made), Root emphatically declined to participate in the perpetuation of the myth of the called shot: "I'm tired of being the goat in that one."

Earl Averill
1929 Cleveland Indians

In 1929, Averill became the first American
Leaguer to hit a home run in his first major-
league at bat. His Cleveland teammates
dubbed him Rockhead when he put himself
on the disabled list by letting a firecracker
explode in his hand, but Earl preferred the
more dignified abbreviation Rock. His dis-
tinguished career earned him a place in the
Hall of Fame, but today he is remembered
mainly for one swing of the bat: In the 1937
All-Star Game, Averill hit a line drive that
broke the big toe on pitcher Dizzy Dean's
left foot.

Dizzy Dean
1938 Chicago Cubs

Dean had pitched more innings than anyone
else in baseball between 1932 and 1936, and
he was already suffering arm problems
when Averill's line drive broke his toe. But
when he returned to the mound before his
injury had healed, Dizzy ruined his arm for
good, and his fastball was gone forever. In
April 1938, Branch Rickey traded Dean to
the Cubs for three players and $185,000.
Dizzy helped the Cubs win the pennant
with his 7–1 record, but he lost Game Two
of the 1938 World Series, despite a valiant
effort: "I never had nothin'. I couldn't break
a pane of glass and I knew it, but I pitched."

   This photograph portends the demise of
baseball's golden age: The Cubs have adopted the zipper.

← Branch Rickey
1914 St. Louis Browns

Catching for the New York Highlanders on June 28, 1907, Branch Rickey set a major-league record when he allowed the Washington Senators to steal thirteen bases. He soon left baseball to become a law student. Conlon photographed Branch upon his return to New York as manager of the Browns.

The Mahatma mystified players with his scholarly approach to baseball and irked them with his stinginess during salary negotiations. He amused the baseball world with such eccentric notions as the pitching machine, the batting cage, and the batting helmet, all of which have, of course, become universally accepted. He later developed the modern minor-league farm system for the St. Louis Cardinals, and, as general manager of the Brooklyn Dodgers, he broke baseball's racist color line by signing a ball player named Jackie Robinson.

Charles Comiskey →
Chicago White Sox Owner, 1917

Before Charley Comiskey revolutionized first-base play in the 1880s, a first baseman planted himself close to the bag and rarely strayed. It occurred to Commy that he could field more ground balls if he stood a few yards away from the base and yet still have time to cover the bag if necessary. There were fears that his unorthodox style of play would confuse his infielders, but the other fellows seem to have caught on.

In 1917, Comiskey was at the Polo Grounds, watching his White Sox win the World Series. Two years later, team members would become fed up with earning the worst wages in baseball from the miserly Comiskey, and the "Black Sox" would take the field for the 1919 World Series.

Heinie Zimmerman
1913 Chicago Cubs

"Heinie Zimmerman is great with the stick this year," reported *The Sporting News* in 1912, "but he has recently brought shame on the national game and the profession of ball playing. At a game in St. Louis, umpire Rigler had occasion to order Zimmerman from the game. The player, instead of leaving the field, is alleged to have gone before the grandstand and so offended decency by his obscene actions that even men were made to blush." Heinie was fined $100, but he went on to win the Triple Crown. Playing third base for the Giants in the 1917 World Series, Zimmerman became the Series goat when he chased a White Sox runner home without throwing the ball, but Heinie pointed out that none of his Giant teammates had covered home plate: "Who the hell was I going to throw the ball to? The umpire?" When Zimmerman and Hal Chase were suspended from baseball in 1919 for fixing games, the editor of *The Sporting News* had to admit that he was sorry to see the colorful Zimmerman go: "He is doubtless uncouth, vulgar, and altogether unreliable, but even so he has some of the qualities that excite a certain sort of admiration."

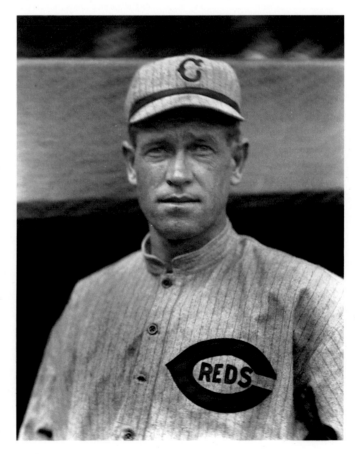

Hal Chase ➡
1917 Cincinnati Reds

Prince Hal was one of the greatest-fielding first basemen in baseball history but he ended up a drunken desert drifter. Why? Because Chase was also the biggest crook in baseball history, the man who made the 1919 Black Sox scandal inevitable. Chase was finally banned from baseball in the wake of that scandal, but by that point he had already been throwing games for more than a decade, and, as Chase himself put it: "Once the evil started, there was no stopping it, and club owners were not strong enough to cope with the evil."

Hal Chase summed up his life on his deathbed: "I am an outcast and I haven't a good name. I'm the loser just like all gamblers are. I lived to make great plays. What did I gain? Nothing. Everything was lost because I raised hell after hours. I was a wise guy, a know-it-all, I guess."

Charles M. Conlon: "Too bad about Hal. But when he *had* it, he had it."

Shoeless Joe Jackson
1913 Cleveland Naps

Conlon gives us a pitcher's-eye view of one of the most fearsome batters ever to step up to the plate, the man who inspired Babe Ruth's batting style. Shoeless Joe is posing at the Polo Grounds during the season when he became the first man ever to hit a ball over the roof of the right-field grandstand and completely out of the park. He holds Black Betsy, his customized Louisville Slugger darkened not by paint, but by fire. No other man ever used such a bat.

Buck Weaver
1916 Chicago White Sox

Ty Cobb called him the greatest third baseman he ever saw, but Buck Weaver was banned from baseball after the Black Sox conspired to lose the 1919 World Series. Weaver was not a participant in the plot, but he did have "guilty knowledge" of it and chose not to inform on his team-mates. For the rest of his life he strug-gled in vain to clear his name.

In the background is the brilliant Black Sox pitcher Eddie Cicotte, who threw the 1919 World Series for $10,000 in cash.

Eddie Cicotte
c. 1913 Chicago White Sox

"I was credited with inventing the knuckler, but at least half the credit belongs to Eddie 'Kickapoo' Summers. Detroit had us both farmed to Indianapolis in 1906 and while there we developed the knuckleball. After I joined the Red Sox in 1908, I acquired the nickname 'Knuckles' on account of the pitch." Conlon made many studies of Cicotte demonstrating his new and peculiar pitching grip. Note that Eddie's knuckles did not touch the ball; the pitch's name arose from the fact that the knuckles were prominently raised above the ball.

But Eddie did not stop at the knuckleball: "All the pitching deliveries concocted by the imagination were tabooed in certain quarters after Cicotte made a success of fooling batters last year," said White Sox manager Pants Rowland in 1918. "They talked about the 'mud ball,' the 'paraffin ball,' the 'licorice ball,' the 'talcum ball,' and about every other kind of delivery." A master of gamesmanship, Cicotte continually rubbed the ball against his uniform and brought it to his mouth, baffling batters with an all-purpose mystery pitch that came to be called the "shine ball."

Eddie Cicotte
c. 1913 Chicago White Sox

Cicotte and his Black Sox teammates were banned from baseball after they nearly destroyed the World Series. More than three decades later, Cicotte was still not fully aware of the gravity of his transgressions: "That was all long, long ago. We done wrong and we deserved to get punished. But not a life sentence. That was too rough."

Ray Schalk
1923 Chicago White Sox

Catcher Ray Schalk pauses to take batting practice, his glove and ball perched on home plate. He had looked on helplessly as his Black Sox teammates deliberately lost the 1919 World Series: "Schalk was wise the moment I started pitching," said Eddie Cicotte. The catcher immediately complained to his manager, Kid Gleason, who in turn complained to Charles Comiskey. But when American League president Ban Johnson was informed of Comiskey's suspicions, he drunkenly dismissed them as "the whelp of a beaten cur."

"It was the Kid who made me a real catcher," said Schalk. "There were mornings when he worked me so hard I thought I'd never be able to crawl out and catch in the afternoon. But you know, I always did. If I was a success it was because of Gleason. He sold me on the idea that a little fellow didn't have to give too much ground to the big bruisers in baseball. What a wonderful little man he was."

Kid Gleason
1926 Philadelphia Athletics

In Ring Lardner's classic baseball book, *You Know Me Al,* White Sox coach Kid Gleason is pitcher Jack Keefe's keeper and taskmaster: "I believe Gleason will starve me to death," complains Jack in a typical moment of self-pity. "A little slob like him don't realize that a big man like I needs good food and plenty of it." The rough-and-tumble Kid became manager of the White Sox in 1919: "We never had no fightin' on that club. I used to tell those mugs that if they wanted to fight, they could fight me. I was no juvenile, but I could move in and go to work in a fight. And we didn't have no fightin' either." But those mugs betrayed him in the World Series, and Gleason realized too late the error of his permissive ways: "I oughta grabbed a bat and crashed it down over the empty skulls of every one of those players." The man in this photograph is recovering from a nervous breakdown; Philadelphia manager Connie Mack has taken pity on the Kid and given his old friend a job.

← Walter Johnson
1927 Washington Senators

Lou Gehrig
1927 New York Yankees

Two of baseball's greatest gentlemen shake hands before a game at Yankee Stadium. Johnson (left) is in his last year as a player, and Gehrig (right) is in his first year as a superstar.

Moe Berg ➡
1935 Boston Red Sox

John Kieran
New York Times Sports Columnist

Kieran was a regular panelist on the popular radio quiz show "Information Please!" When Moe Berg appeared as a guest on the program, the catcher astounded listeners coast to coast with the depth of his erudition. Kieran, an expert ornithologist, was often accompanied by Berg on New York nature walks.

Orval Overall
1910 Chicago Cubs

The last time the Cubs won a world championship, Orval was the pitcher who clinched it by shutting down Ty Cobb and the Detroit Tigers in 1908. In that final game, he struck out four men in one inning, the first and only time that feat has been accomplished in World Series play. Overall's baseball career was cut short by arm troubles, but he later became a successful banker.

Johnny Kling
1913 Cincinnati Reds

After the Cubs won the 1908 World Series, catcher Johnny Kling decided to hold out for a big raise in 1909. This was a big mistake. The president of the Cubs reminded Kling that Marshall Field, the founder of Chicago's famous department store, had passed away only a few years earlier: "That store will go on just as if nothing happened," he said, "and so will the Cubs if you stay out." Johnny stayed out and the Cubs went on just as if nothing had happened, with Jimmy Archer behind the plate. Kling gave pocket billiard exhibitions before meekly returning to the Cubs in 1910.

In their retirement years, many Chicago catchers shared the same uncanny fate: Ray Schalk of the White Sox and Johnny Kling, Jimmy Archer, Gabby Hartnett, and Bob O'Farrell of the Cubs all became prosperous owners of bowling alleys.

← Lee Meadows
1924 Pittsburgh Pirates

In 1921, pitcher Lee Meadows disagreed with a strike call by umpire Bill Brennan. Removing his glasses, he approached the umpire and offered them to him: "You need these worse than I do, Bill." A former botany instructor, Meadows was the first ball player to wear glasses in the twentieth century. Since he was a pitcher, standing only 60'6" from home plate, skeptics warned him that he was making a brave but particularly foolhardy career choice for one so "afflicted." In 1920, a batted ball did indeed strike Meadows in the face, shattering his spectacles, but fortunately this batting-practice foul ball left him with no permanent injuries.

When his playing days were over Lee went to work for the IRS.

Fred Luderus →
1915 Philadelphia Phillies

Slugging team captain Luderus led all Philadelphia batters with a .438 average in the 1915 World Series, a performance that earned him a Coca-Cola endorsement in 1916. Grover Cleveland Alexander had three consecutive thirty-game-winning seasons for the Phillies with Luderus at first base, and he remembered his old teammate fondly: "Fred'd come up to me before a game and say, 'Well, boy, you get out there and I'll try and get a couple for you.' Maybe he'd hit two up against the fence, maybe he wouldn't. But if he didn't, he didn't. No sense in worrying. Ball players never worried in the old days."

Red Ruffing
1926 Boston Red Sox

By 1929, one apoplectic Boston sportswriter had seen enough: "Ruffing is nothing but a snare and a delusion and a bitter disappointment as a right-handed pitcher. He would add to the strength of the team by not going into the box at all. There
is nothing mysterious about this, as Charley loses all his games. It ought not to be
difficult to replace a pitcher who loses all his games." Sadly, this was not much of
an exaggeration: Ruffing lost seven out of every ten of his decisions with the Red
Sox. But what could you expect from a pitcher who was missing four toes on his
left foot after an accident in a coal mine?

Red Ruffing
1936 New York Yankees

By 1936, Red was a twenty-game winner
destined for the Hall of Fame.

Mel Ott
1928 New York Giants

In 1928, his third year as a Giant, nineteen-year-old Mel Ott finally put his home-run swing on display. He would go on to lead the National League in home runs six times. When he retired in 1947, he had hit more home runs than any other batter in National League history. Conlon was living dangerously when he stood in the range of this pull hitter during batting practice, but the result was one of his most beautiful photographs.

Mel Ott
1933 New York Giants

"The biggest kick I ever got came in the 1933 World Series." In this, his first World Series, Ott hit a home run in his first at bat, went four for four in his first game, and won the Series with a tenth-inning home run in Game Five.

On December 6, 1941, Ott succeeded Bill Terry as manager of the Giants. Brooklyn manager Leo Durocher conceded that there had never been a nicer guy than Mel Ott, but he qualified his praise for the Giant manager with these immortal words: "Nice guys finish last."

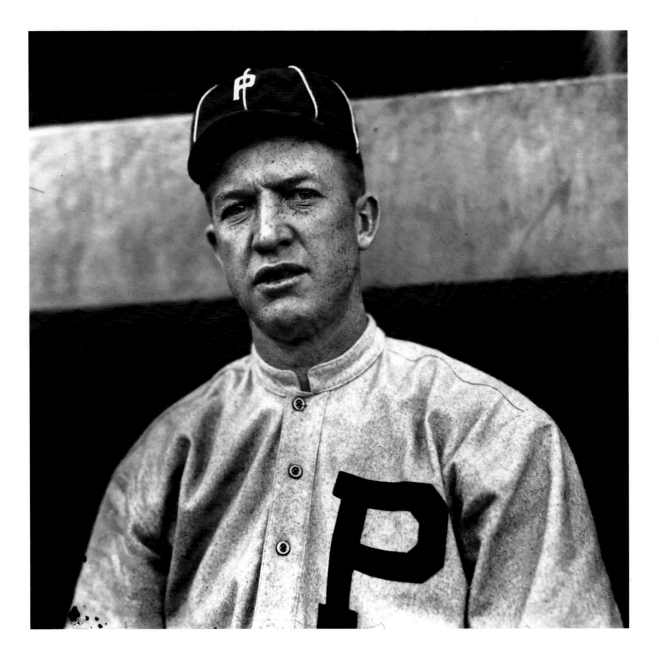

Grover Cleveland Alexander
1915 Philadelphia Phillies

In 1915, the twenty-eight-year-old Alexander won thirty-one games, leading the Phillies to the World Series. The next year he won thirty-three games, and thirty more the year after that. His 1916 total of sixteen shutouts is still the all-time major-league record. When he retired with 373 victories in 1930, he had tied Christy Mathewson for third place on the all-time list.

Grover Cleveland Alexander
1928 St. Louis Cardinals

Once the greatest pitcher alive, in his last years Alexander was an unspeakably tragic figure, destitute and ravaged by alcohol: "I'm in the Hall of Fame at Cooperstown, New York, and I'm proud to be there," he said in 1944, "but I can't eat the Hall of Fame. And I can't eat the promises of jobs that I get every day and never materialize. I can drink all the beer I want for nothing—I can get enough in one day to keep me drunk for a week if I wanted to do that—but I can't get a bite to eat."

Babe Ruth
1922 New York Yankees

In 1922, the Babe was fuming. He missed the first five weeks of the season after being suspended for an unauthorized barnstorming trip. Five days after his return, he threw a handful of dirt into an umpire's face, chased a fan into the stands, and was suspended again. Run-ins with umpires Big Bill Dinneen and Tommy Connolly resulted in three more suspensions, rousing Ban Johnson to this blunt warning: "A man of your stamp bodes no good in the profession. The time has arrived when you should allow some intelligence to creep into a mind that has plainly been warped." After the season, Ruth vowed that he would change his ways. The next year he won the American League Most Valuable Player award.

Babe Ruth
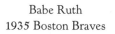
1935 Boston Braves

Playing for Boston, the city where it all began for him in 1914, a washed-up ballplayer makes his farewell appearance in New York. The Babe hit his last three home runs in a game against Pittsburgh on May 25, 1935, but his instinct for the dramatic failed him, and he did not bow out of baseball with this electrifying performance. One long week later, he finally retired.

Zack Wheat, Jr., and Zack Wheat
1925 Brooklyn Dodgers

Zack and Daisy Wheat lived near Ebbets Field and took their kids to all the
Dodger games. Here Zack poses for Conlon with his son, wearing a black arm-
band in memory of the recently deceased Dodger owner, Charles Ebbets. Mrs.
Wheat had an especially memorable day at Ebbets Field in 1925: When Zack
broke a scoreless tie with a home run in the bottom of the ninth, the fan seat-
ed next to Daisy dropped dead.

Sam Leslie and Sam Leslie, Jr.
1935 Brooklyn Dodgers

Leslie had twenty-two pinch hits in 1932, setting a major-league record that
would stand for nearly three decades, and he batted .500 as a pinch hitter for
the New York Giants in the 1936 and 1937 World Series. Here the tools of
ignorance overwhelm his tiny son.

← Ed Walsh
1912 Chicago White Sox

Big Ed had his last great season in 1912 when he won twenty-seven games for the second year in a row. By 1913 his arm was dead, his career virtually over. He had simply thrown too many pitches: Between 1906 and 1912, Walsh averaged nearly 360 innings a season, the equivalent of forty complete games a year.

He later served briefly and unhappily as an American League umpire and was the pitching coach at the University of Notre Dame when his son Ed, Jr., pitched there in the mid-1920s.

→ Ed Walsh, Jr.
1928 Chicago White Sox

Twenty-three-year-old rookie Ed Walsh, Jr., is breaking into the majors with the White Sox at the same age his father did. Unfortunately, this is where their career parallels end. How did it feel to be the son of the illustrious Ed Walsh? "Terrible. Being the son of a great man is a rotten handicap." Young Ed's major-league career was forgettable at best, and he was dead at the age of thirty-two, the victim of rheumatic fever. But he did accomplish one unforgettable feat: He stopped Joe DiMaggio's longest batting streak. On July 26, 1933, pitching in the Pacific Coast League, Ed Walsh, Jr., held the eighteen-year-old DiMaggio hitless after Joe had batted safely in sixty-one consecutive games.

Paul Dean and Dizzy Dean
1934 St. Louis Cardinals

When Dizzy (right) predicted before the 1934 season that "me 'n' Paul" would win forty-five games between them, it was regarded as just another of his outrageous boasts. But the Deans surpassed this figure with forty-nine wins during the season, and each won two more games in the World Series. It was the greatest year two pitching brothers ever had.

Wes Ferrell and Rick Ferrell
1935 Boston Red Sox

Meet the proprietors and purveyors of the Ferrell Brothers' Big League Dog Food and the best brother battery in the history of baseball. On July 19, 1933, Wes Ferrell (left) was pitching for the Indians when Red Sox catcher Rick Ferrell (right), hit a home run. Wes berated Rick as the latter ran around the bases: How dare he hit a home run off his own flesh and blood? When the umpire gave Wes a new baseball, he immediately drop-kicked it into the stands. Wes was still livid when he came up to bat in the bottom of the inning, and, ignoring a bunt sign, *he* now hit a home run. Wes Ferrell still holds the major-league record for career home runs by a pitcher.

← Paul Waner and Lloyd Waner
1927 Pittsburgh Pirates

At the Polo Grounds in 1927, a sports-writer heard a fan with a Brooklyn accent loudly proclaiming his admira-tion for the big person, Paul (left), and the little person, Lloyd (right). Here are Big Poison and Little Poison, posing for Conlon at the Polo Grounds during the greatest year two brothers ever had. Playing side by side in the outfield, Paul and Lloyd had 460 hits between them, with a combined batting average of .367. Their efforts got them into the 1927 World Series, but neither ever played in the Fall Classic again.

Pinky Hargrave →
1930 Detroit Tigers

Bubbles Hargrave
1930 New York Yankees

Here is a typical Conlon pose with a charming twist: two catchers, two bro-thers. Bubbles (right) led the National League in batting in 1926, the first time in the 1920s that Rogers Hornsby failed to win the batting crown, and the first time in the twentieth century that a catcher won a batting title. Pinky (left) was a red-haired journeyman who raised beagles in his spare time.

174

Rube Waddell
1905 Philadelphia Athletics

Conlon was the only photographer able to capture the mad gleam in the eye of this adult child bewitched by windup toys and whiskey, fire trucks and floozies. Waddell was a masterful pitcher who could strike out batters at will, but he was also a demented brat: "Sometimes when a batter bunted in the vicinity of the pitcher's box," recalled a teammate, "the Rube would reach for the ball but instead would grab his own foot, turn it over, and yell that his ankle was broken." In 1904, Waddell struck out 349 batters, a major-league record that would not be approached for decades. But Rube was literally unmanageable, and Connie Mack traded his star pitcher away after the 1907 season. He died at thirty-seven, a victim of alcoholism and tuberculosis.

Connie Mack →
1929 Philadelphia Athletics

"Mr. Mack doesn't have to open his mouth," said Al Simmons. "A wave of that scorecard is enough." When Connie Mack celebrated his fiftieth anniversary as a major-league manager in 1944, President Franklin D. Roosevelt sent him a telegram: "Long may your scorecard wave." In 1929, Mack was waving his A's to their first World Series in fifteen years.

Lou Gehrig
1934 New York Yankees

In 1934, the Iron Horse led the major leagues with a career-high forty-nine home runs and became the first Yankee ever to win the Triple Crown.

Johnny Mize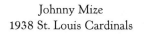
1938 St. Louis Cardinals

The Big Cat peers down at Conlon with the look of sleepy self-assurance that earned him his nickname. Mize, whose cousin Claire was Babe Ruth's second wife, led the National League in home runs four times. He spent the last five years of his career as a Yankee first baseman, and in each of those years the Yankees won the World Series.

Fielder Jones
1904 Chicago White Sox

This man's prescient parents chris-
tened him Fielder Allison Jones when
he was born in Shinglehouse, Penn-
sylvania, in 1874. He was the center
fielder and manager of the White Sox,
leading the Hitless Wonders to a
world championship in 1906. But
Jones was a very hard loser, and in
1918, when he had been reduced to
managing the dismal St. Louis Browns,
Fielder finally snapped. After a particularly tough loss, a club official said
innocently: "Goodbye, see you tomor-
row," to which the seething Jones
replied: "I don't think you will. Not
unless you come out to the Pacific
Ocean. I'm going home." He left the
team and returned to his Oregon lum-
ber business, quitting baseball forever.

Al Schacht
1928 Washington Senators

These twinkling eyes belong to the Clown Prince of Baseball, the slapstick comic who entertained fans in ballparks around the world for decades, wearing a battered top hat and swallowtail coat. Conlon photographed Schacht's alternate persona, the respected third-base coach of the Washington Senators. In 1908, the fifteen-year-old Schacht had sold peanuts and soda pop at the Polo Grounds in order to be near his idols, Turkey Mike Donlin and Christy Mathewson. By 1911, he was the Giants' batting-practice pitcher, learning Matty's fadeaway from the master himself. Schacht pitched briefly for the Senators before an arm injury ended his career.

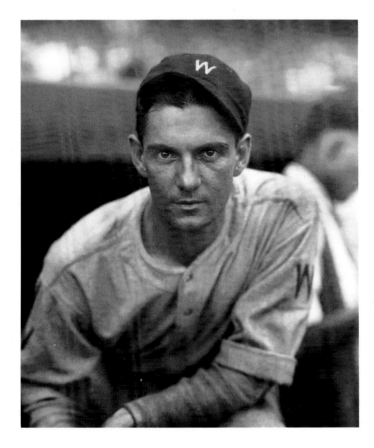

↑

Carl Mays
1922 New York Yankees

Mays was a brilliant pitcher with a spectacular submarine delivery, but he was despised by teammates and opponents alike because of his foul personality. He did little to improve their opinion of him when, on August 16, 1920, he threw the pitch that killed the popular Cleveland shortstop Ray Chapman.

Tommy Connolly
American League Umpire, c. 1913

Connolly, born in Manchester, England, began his umpiring career in New England in 1894. He was the very first American League umpire—his was the only game not rained out on Opening Day in 1901—and he umpired the first World Series in 1903. Tommy gave misbehaving players fair warning when the limits of his tolerance had been reached: "You can go so far with Connolly," said Ty Cobb, "but when you see his neck get red, it's time to lay off of him." And he always had the last word in any dispute: "I may be wrong, but I'm right officially. Play ball!"

Connolly was behind home plate when Carl Mays threw the pitch that killed Ray Chapman. Mays accused the umpire of causing the tragedy by failing to remove a scuffed baseball from play. The pitcher, of course, had scuffed the ball in the first place.

Muddy Ruel
1924 Washington Senators

"Muddy made a pitcher out of me when I was all through," said Walter Johnson. "He was the smartest catcher baseball ever had, and certainly the greatest handler of pitchers. When I worked with Muddy, it was like sitting in a rocking chair. I never disputed his choice of pitches." Ruel, a practicing attorney who scored the winning run in the 1924 World Series, was nicknamed Muddy by childhood playmates after he made a spectacular rainy-day slide into a mudhole.

Ruel was the catcher behind the plate when Carl Mays threw the pitch that killed Ray Chapman.

←

Ray Chapman   →
1917 Cleveland Indians

In 1917, the world mourned the tragic death of Cleveland's famous canine mascot, Larry. For many years, Larry had shared hotel accommodations on the road with Jack Graney and Graney's human roommate, Ray Chapman.

Today Chapman is a morbid footnote, famous only for the manner of his death. But once upon a time he was "Chappie," a talented all-around ball player and a singer in the ball club barbershop quartet, a happy-go-lucky fellow who would join his Cleveland teammates before a game as they lined up in single file, leaned over and let Larry bound across their backs.

Ty Cobb
1910 Detroit Tigers

The Sporting News reported in 1910: "Cobb, it seems, is unpopular with the masses in general, and especially with the players, and it is all brought about by his great love for Ty Cobb himself. But withal, you have to acknowledge that he is the greatest ball player in the game today and possibly the greatest of all time. Hate this marvel if you wish—what cares he? The greater your hate for him, the harder he will play ball."

The St. Louis Browns made manifest their hatred for Cobb on October 9, 1910, when they conspired to "lay down" for Napoleon Lajoie, Cobb's opponent for the batting title. With the assistance of the Browns, the well-liked Lajoie went eight for eight, forever clouding the results of the 1910 batting race. It was diplomatically declared a tie, and both players were awarded Chalmers automobiles.

Ty Cobb
1928 Philadelphia Athletics

Conlon's 1910 photograph of Cobb appeared annually in the baseball guides for the next decade. The perennial American League batting champion took great pride in the fact that his batting stance remained unchanged throughout his twenty-four-year career, and indeed, although separated in time by nearly two decades, these two Conlon images eerily mirror one another.

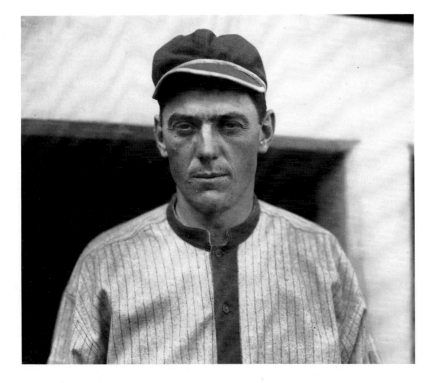

Clyde Milan
1940 Washington Senators   ↓

"Center field was sun field in Washington, and I played there mostly. The old type sun glasses were not satisfactory to me. You had to keep them over your eyes all the time, and that annoyed me. I lost more fly balls with glasses than without them, so I said to heck with them. I would play a ball hit into the glare by shading my eye with my glove." Decades of staring into the sun gave Clyde the most amazing set of wrinkles ever seen at a ballpark. He spent his last morning on earth hitting spring-training fungoes in the Florida sunshine. When he went inside to the Senators' clubhouse, Clyde collapsed and died.

↑

Clyde Milan
1913 Washington Senators

When Ty Cobb stole ninety-six bases in 1915, setting a major-league record that would stand for nearly fifty years, he surpassed Clyde Milan's record 1912 total of eighty-eight. Clyde had great respect for his main competitor on the base-paths: "Ty was tops. He had the nervous foot of the born stealer. He never liked the base he was on. I was geared the same way—the bag ahead always looked more attractive."

In 1907, Clyde Milan and Walter Johnson were discovered by the Senators during the same scouting trip. They joined the team within a month of each other and were roommates for fourteen years.

↑

Dutch Leonard
1914 Boston Red Sox

Leonard's 1914 earned run average of 1.01 is still the best in major-league history. In 1915, Dutch made a lifelong enemy of Ty Cobb by intentionally hitting him with a pitch. Cobb retaliated by trying to spike the Red Sox pitcher. Leonard had his revenge in 1926 when he implicated Cobb, Tris Speaker, and Smokey Joe Wood in a game-fixing conspiracy, provoking a scandal that nearly resulted in the players' expulsion from baseball. Leonard refused to level his charges in Cobb's presence, preferring instead to remain in the safety of his California raisin ranch. This was a wise move, since Cobb very likely would have strangled his accuser. The charges were dropped, but the taint remained.

Earl Whitehill ↓
1924 Detroit Tigers

In 1924, Earl met his future bride, Violet Oliver, the California girl who appears on the Sun-Maid raisin box. Whitehill's stunning good looks were the object of taunts by opposing bench jockeys who hoped to capitalize on his violent temper: He once threw the home plate umpire's whisk broom over the grandstand after a disputed call. Even Tiger manager Ty Cobb was wary of antagonizing the volatile southpaw. Whitehill has the worst lifetime earned run average of any pitcher with 200 or more wins, which may help to explain his extreme irascibility.

John McGraw
1909 New York Giants

Christy Mathewson: "Did you ever see the little manager crouching, immovable, at third base with a mitt on his hand, when the New York club goes to bat in the seventh inning two runs behind? The first batter gets a base on balls. McGraw leaps into the air, kicks his heels together, claps his mitt, shouts at the umpire, runs in and pats the next batter on the back, and says something to the pitcher. The crowd gets its cue, wakes up and leaps into the air, kicking its heels together. The whole atmosphere inside the park is changed in a minute, and the air is bristling with enthusiasm. The game has found Ponce de Leon's fountain of youth, and the little, silent actor on the third base coaching line is the cause of the change."

Christy Mathewson →
1911 New York Giants

Mathewson was Conlon's first and favorite subject. In 1937, the photographer recalled his old friend: "I treasured Matty's confidence. In 1911, I went to the World Series in Philadelphia. Coming back to New York, I dived into the diner at North Philadelphia. I sat down at a table for four. Soon, in came Matty, [former Giant catcher Roger] Bresnahan, and [Giant pitcher Hooks] Wiltse. They began to discuss the game—what had happened and why, what would have or might have happened. They discussed fellow players in a frank way. Matty did, anyway. Bresnahan gave him an inquiring look. Matty looked at me, with a smile. He said, 'Roger, Charley can be trusted—always.' I got one of the biggest kicks of my life out of that remark."

189

← Willard Hershberger
1939 Cincinnati Reds

Willard Hershberger is the only major-league player to kill himself during the season. He was a substitute catcher called into action during an intense heat wave and an equally intense pennant race. On August 3, 1940, blaming himself for Reds losses, Hershberger leaned over a hotel bathtub and slashed his throat. When the Reds won the 1940 World Series, they voted Hershberger's mother a full share of their earnings, nearly $6000.

Ginger Beaumont →
1910 Chicago Cubs

Ginger was the first man ever to bat in the World Series when he flied out against Cy Young in 1903. He was also the first man to go 0 for 5. In 1902, he led the National League in batting, beating out players like Honus Wagner, Wee Willie Keeler, and Wahoo Sam Crawford. It is fitting that Ginger made his last major-league appearance in the 1910 World Series, when he walked and scored a run to end his career.

192

Topsy Hartsel
1909 Philadelphia Athletics

Hartsel was the speedy Athletics lead-off man in the first decade of this century whose diminutive stature (5′ 5″) helped him lead the league in walks five times. His teammates nicknamed him after a black character in *Uncle Tom's Cabin* because they thought he looked like an albino. In turn-of-the-century white America, this was considered a very funny joke.

Bill Dickey
1928 New York Yankees

Here is an unknown rookie catcher who played in only ten games for the Yankees in 1928. Of course, Bill Dickey went on to become one of the greatest Yankees of all time, but this example illustrates Conlon's approach to his subjects: Take every player's picture, no matter how brief his stay in the big leagues. Dickey never got to play in the 1928 World Series, but at least this photograph made it into the 1928 World Series souvenir program.

← Chick Hafey
1929 St. Louis Cardinals

In this wistful portrait, a man is finally getting a good look at the world. Hafey was plagued by chronic sinus and eye ailments. Surgery provided little relief, but when he put on glasses for the first time in 1929, Hafey was delighted: He could now watch movies without getting a headache. Chick became the first batting champion to wear glasses and was the first bespectacled Hall of Famer, but bright days never ceased to plague him, even with the flip-up sun glasses he wore under the bill of his cap.

Big Bill Dinneen →
American League Umpire, 1910

Dinneen was the pitching hero of the very first World Series, in 1903, when he won three games and led the Boston Pilgrims to victory over the Pittsburgh Pirates. He retired as a player near the end of the 1909 season and immediately became an umpire, beginning a new career that would last until 1937. Conlon spotted a reflective Dinneen preparing for a game at Hilltop Park during his first full season as an umpire.

Hack Simmons
1910 Detroit Tigers

George Washington Simmons was a baseball nonentity, a mediocre utility man who bounced back and forth between the majors and minors throughout his brief career. But one afternoon he leapt for Charles M. Conlon, and he hasn't come back to earth yet. He is still there with Cobb and Crawford at Hilltop Park, still there floating over the field of dreams.

INDEX TO THE PLATES